HOW STARBUCKS
SAVED MY LIFE

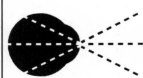

This Large Print Book carries the
Seal of Approval of N.A.V.H.

HOW STARBUCKS SAVED MY LIFE

A SON OF PRIVILEGE LEARNS TO LIVE LIKE EVERYONE ELSE

MICHAEL GATES GILL

THORNDIKE PRESS

An imprint of Thomson Gale, a part of The Thomson Corporation

THOMSON
™
GALE

Detroit • New York • San Francisco • New Haven, Conn. • Waterville, Maine • London

L.T.E.
647.95092
G475

LIBRARY OF CONGRESS CATALOGING-IN-PUBLICATION DATA

Gill, Michael (Michael Gates)
    How Starbucks saved my life : a son of privilege learns to live like everyone else / by Michael Gates Gill. — Large print ed.
        p. cm. — (Thorndike Press large print biography)
    Originally published: New York : Gotham Books, c2007.
    ISBN-13: 978-1-4104-0360-5 (hardcover : alk. paper)
    ISBN-10: 1-4104-0360-2 (hardcover : alk. paper)
    1. Gill, Michael (Michael Gates) 2. Advertising executives — New York (State) — New York — Biography. 3. Marketing consultants — New York (State) — New York — Biography. 4. Starbucks Coffee Company — Employees — New York (State) — New York — Biography. 5. Coffeehouses — New York (State) — New York. 6. Acoustic neuroma — Patients — United States — Biography. 7. Large type books. I. Title.
    CT275.G4163A3 2007b
    647.95092—dc22
    [B]   2007035716

Published in 2008 by arrangement with Gotham Books, a member of Penguin Group (USA) Inc.

Printed in the United States of America on permanent paper
10 9 8 7 6 5 4 3 2 1

To my children,
with gratitude for
their understanding hearts

1
FROM DRINKING
LATTES TO SERVING
THEM UP

"The humble improve."
— a quote from Wynton Marsalis, jazz
musician, published on the side of a cup
of a Starbucks Double Tall Skim Latte

This is the true, surprising story of an old white man who was kicked out of the top of the American Establishment, by chance met a young African-American woman from a completely different background, and came to learn what is important in life. He was born into privilege on the affluent Upper East Side of Manhattan, she into poverty in the projects in Brooklyn. He once had a high-powered advertising job and now had nothing; she came from the streets and now had succeeded — so much so that she was able to offer a stranger a chance to save himself.

This is *my* story, and like all surprising stories, it starts with an accident.

7

March

I should not have been anywhere near the location of that transforming experience. But on that particular rainy day in March of last year, I could not resist the urge to go back in time.

Have you ever wanted — when life is too hard to bear — to return to the comfort of your childhood home? I had been the only son of adoring if often absent parents, and now I wanted to recapture some sense of the favored place I had once occupied in the universe. I found myself back on East Seventy-eighth Street, staring across at the four-story brownstone where I had grown up.

I had a sudden image of a crane hoisting a Steinway grand piano into the second-floor living room. My mother had decided I should learn to play the piano, and my father had thrown himself into the project. Nothing was too good for his only son, and he had rushed out and bought the biggest, most expensive model. After the purchase of the huge Steinway, the problem became how to get this magnificent instrument into our home, a hundred-year-old house with narrow, steep stairs.

My father had been up to the challenge.

He hired a crane, and then had the men raise it up to the second floor, where, by opening the French windows, and turning the piano on its side, they could just make it fit. My father had been terribly proud of his accomplishment and my mother delighted. Of course, I had been secretly happy to be the reason for all this unusual activity.

Today, as I gazed at the stately building that had once been my home, I thought of how much all of that extravagant effort must have cost. How far I had fallen from those happy times. I had come a long way from my childhood, when money was never mentioned. I was now nearly broke.

Turning away from the comforts of the past, I looked for some comfort in a latte. One of my last remaining treats. A Starbucks store now occupied the corner of Lexington and Seventy-eighth, where during my childhood there had been a pastry shop. In my depressed daze, I did not notice the sign in front reading: "Hiring Open House" — not that it was the kind of sign that I would have noticed anyway. Later, I was to learn that Starbucks has hiring events at different stores every week or so in New York. Managers from other stores in the area come in to interview prospective employees. Looking back now, I realize that the good fortune that had left my life returned the moment I chose to step into the store at the corner of Seventy-eighth Street.

Still in my own cocoon of self-pity and nostalgia about lost fortune and family, I ordered my latte and made my way over to a small table. I sat down and did not look at anyone nearby. Staring into my interior space, I tried to make sense of a life that seemed to have completely gotten away from me.

"Would you like a job?"

I was startled out of my reverie. The speaker sat at the table right next to mine, shuffling some papers with professional dispatch. She was an attractive young African-American woman wearing a Starbucks uniform. I had not even looked at her before, but now I noticed she was wearing a silver bracelet and a fancy watch. She seemed so secure and confident.

I was struck numb. I wasn't used to interacting with *anyone* in Starbucks. For the last few months I had been frequenting many Starbucks stores around in the city, not as places to relax or chat, but as "offices" where I could call prospective clients — although none were now answering my calls. My little consulting company was rapidly going downhill. Marketing and advertising is a young man's business, and at sixty-three, I had found that my efforts were met with a deafening silence.

"A job," the woman repeated again, smiling, as if I hadn't heard her. "Would you like one?"

Was I that transparent? Despite my pin-striped Brooks Brothers suit and Master of the Universe manner — I had my cell phone resting on top of my expensive leather T. Anthony briefcase as if expecting an important call — could she see that I was really one of life's losers? Did I, a former creative director of J. Walter Thompson Company, the largest advertising agency in the world, want a job at *Starbucks?!*

For one of the few times in my life, I could not think of a polite lie or any answer but the truth.

"Yes," I said without thinking, "I *would* like a job."

I'd never had to seek a job before. After commencement at Yale in 1963, I'd gotten a call from James Henry Brewster, IV, a friend of mine in Skull & Bones.

"Gates," he said assertively, "I'm setting you up at J. Walter Thompson."

Jim was working for Pan Am Airways, the

largest airline in the world at the time, and a major client of J. Walter Thompson's, the advertising firm known as JWT in the business. The two of us had a good time together at college — wouldn't it be a gas to work together now!

Jim set up the interview. When I went in to meet the people at JWT, I was confident of my chances. Not only did I have the "in" through Jim, but the owner of JWT, Stanley Resor, was another Yale man. His son, Stanley Resor, Jr., had roomed with an uncle of mine at Yale. I had visited the Resor family at their two-thousand-acre ranch out at Jackson Hole just the summer before.

These connections proved invaluable. Advertising was regarded as a glamorous profession. Television commercials had just taken off, and become humorous and interesting. Lots of people wanted to get into a business in which you could make plenty of money but also have a creative edge. JWT's training program was regarded as the best in the business, and it hired only one or two copywriters a year.

I was one of those hires.

It had been love at first sight. All I had to do was talk and write — skills that came naturally to me — and they paid me amazingly well for it. I was good at my job, and the clients appreciated my creative ideas.

I also found that I enjoyed making presentations, and doing them in original ways to bring some life and laughter into what could be really boring meetings. For example, because we had created the line "The Marines are looking for a few good men," we were asked to pitch for the Department of Defense's multimillion-dollar recruiting account. The presentation was held in a war room at the Pentagon. As I walked in, I saw a row of bemedaled men sitting behind a high table. These were the Joint Chiefs of Staff. They sat like stone statues, clearly unhappy that they had been dragged into such a frivolous marketing meeting.

I walked up to the front of the room, carrying my portfolio case. I reached inside and pulled out a bow and arrow. Someone else from my team walked to the opposite end of the room with a target I had drawn with Magic Marker on a piece of Styrofoam. I wanted to dramatize the fact that we believed in targeted advertising. I wanted to speak with a tool to which these military men would relate: a weapon. I also wanted to make sure that since we were the first of thirteen agencies these men would be seeing, they would remember us.

I pulled back the arrow, and let it go. By

the grace of God, it hit the bull's-eye. For a minute there was dead silence in that room. No one moved. No one spoke. Then all four military leaders broke into applause, and there were a few cheers, and laughter. We won the account.

In addition to liking the work, I worked extremely hard. There was a sign-in sheet in the lobby of the JWT office building in New York, and I always tried to be one of the first to sign in and one of the last to sign out. I received promotions early and often, moving from copywriter to creative director and executive vice president on a host of major accounts, including Ford, Burger King, Christian Dior, the United States Marine Corps, and IBM.

I was willing to go anywhere to help our clients. JWT was an international company that expected you to be willing to travel nationally and internationally. I had no hesitation in uprooting my growing family — somehow between ads I had found time to marry, have a two-week honeymoon and, in due course, four children — moving to work in offices in Toronto, Washington, D.C., and Los Angeles. I looked at work as a big part of my role of being a good provider for them. When it came to family, no sacrifice was too much. As such, JWT became my top priority.

Yet, in a terrible irony, I flew many hundreds of thousands of miles to spend time with clients, and hardly saw my children. My clients became my children, and my children grew up without me. Was that really my pudgy baby, Annie, now a beautiful young woman graduating from *high school?* It brought tears to my eyes to see her accept her diploma, looking so grown-up and so ready to leave home, and leave me. I realized with a pained clarity that I had missed so many precious moments with her, and with all my children.

And yet I convinced myself — even then — that the sacrifice was worth it, because JWT had supported me. My salary was high and my benefits were excellent, so now that the kids were moving on to college and the bills were about to become even more insane, I didn't need to be terribly concerned. In the back of my mind, I even congratulated myself: *This is why you were smart to dedicate yourself to one company — the stability and the pay.* Like many men of my generation accepting of the role of "breadwinner," I rationalized my devotion to work and trust in JWT.

Loyal to a fault, I worked even longer hours, always ready to adjust my personal schedule for my clients' needs. I remember getting a phone call from the Ford client one Christmas Day when my kids were little. I had just been getting ready to spend a rare day at home, having a chance to play with Elizabeth, Annie, Laura, and Charles and enjoy a few relaxed moments of being a real family, and being a real family man. The client wanted to do a New Year's sale event, and could I shoot some commercials? Ford loved beating up on the agency, and since they spent millions of dollars on ads, they never made you an offer you could safely refuse if you valued your job.

"Sure," I answered. "When?"

"Now," he said.

I heard those emphatic words and knew I had to go, leaving my children in tears. Their presents were just unwrapped, spread out on the living room floor, and everyone was still in their pj's. But I was a loyal JWT man. I got a taxi to the airport and flew to Detroit.

I was full of pride that I had never refused any effort JWT ever asked of me. It was a true shock, then, when twenty-five years into my career, I received a call from young Linda White, a senior JWT executive.

"Let's have breakfast tomorrow," came her directive.

Those aren't good words to hear from a colleague. I liked Linda. A few years earlier, I had convinced the old boy network that we needed an intelligent young woman. Linda had done well, and I had helped get her on the Board of Directors. The only woman on the board. In fact, Linda was now president, having passed me in the corporate hierarchy.

She was a favorite of the new owner of JWT, a Brit named Martin Sorrell whose bookkeeper background made him particularly attentive to the bottom line. Before Martin arrived, JWT was almost like a nonprofit organization, dedicated to doing the best communications for our clients and not worrying about the bottom line. Martin had a different idea. He told the stockholders he was more interested in boosting their profits than in spending to achieve the highest caliber work. He made a hostile bid for our company. We fought him, but Martin had the Wall Street bean counters on his side, and he easily prevailed.

I had been in a meeting when Martin said bluntly, "I like young people around me." I really should have listened to him and seen what was coming.

Martin himself was only in his early forties. Linda was in her early thirties. No wonder they got along. Young, smart people, they were eager to get rid of whom they probably felt were "the old farts."

On the morning of our breakfast, Linda showed up late. Another bad sign. In corporate America, the higher your status, the tardier you are. Consciously or unconsciously, Linda had adopted the style.

She had red eyes. It looked like she had been crying. Yet another bad sign. I knew that Linda liked me and felt some gratitude to me for helping her career, but I also knew that in modern corporate life there was no time for sentimentality. The facts that I was still good at my job, and was honest, and had spent my whole adult life helping JWT become successful were irrelevant.

I had met Linda at a party. She had just graduated with an MBA from Harvard and held an undergraduate degree in history of art. As I told her, it was a winning combination in advertising — she would be strong in creative ideas, while making sure the whole process made a profit. And I had been right. But her credentials alone would not have gotten Linda hired. I had to present her as more macho than any other guy we could hire. In helping Linda move into the top management of JWT, I had written a memo describing her as an "unforgiving high achiever." I had shown the memo to Linda.

"Am I really that unforgiving?" Linda asked me, almost hurt.

"No, maybe not," I said. "But as a female high achiever you have got to be perceived as tough as any male — especially in management. Probably tougher than you really are underneath. Macho number crunching, including crunching people, is the management style Martin really likes."

I had helped Linda focus on the hard substance of the business: money, and an unforgiving attitude toward cutting "overhead" — which in advertising was always people. Now the overhead was *me*.

I smiled at her over the table. I wasn't going to cry. Yet I felt like dying. My heart actually hurt. Was I having a heart attack? No, I just felt really, really sad. And angry with myself. Why hadn't I seen the signs? Linda went forward and upward in her career at JWT; I stayed in place. Linda passed me flying. Martin liked Linda. In a polite, British way, it was clear Martin could not stand being in the same room with me. With my sparse white hair, I was an embarrassment to the kind of lean, mean, hard-charging, young company he wanted to run.

"Michael," Linda said, "I have some bad

news." I fiddled with my muffin, willing myself to meet her eye.

The waiter came up to me to see if we needed anything else. Waiters still think that the old guys have the money and run the show.

I shook my head, and he backed off.

"Let me have it," I said stoically. I wasn't going to beg for mercy. I knew it would not do any good. I hoped that Linda had at least argued for me, for old times' sake. But by the time you got to a breakfast meeting, outside the office, the deal was done. I knew I was history.

"We have to let you go, Michael." She pronounced the words robotically. To her credit, she had a hard time getting them out, especially that phony corporate "we."

"It's not my decision," she hastened to add, and a tear started down her cheek. She brushed it quickly away, embarrassed by her own emotion — particularly in front of a guy who had taught her to be so tough. I don't think she was acting. I think she was genuinely unhappy that I had been fired, and that she had been chosen to do the dirty deed. From the bottom-line point of view, it was, as they said, a "no-brainer." Plenty of young people could write and speak as quickly and well as me — for a quarter of the cost. If Linda had refused to fire me, then she could not be part of the management mafia. It was a test of where her loyalty lay: to an old creative guy who had helped her in the past, or to a young financial whiz who now ran the company? Linda had to prove to Martin that she was unforgiving. You had to kill to get in the mafia. Linda would make her bones this day.

I was brave as I could be. At least for those few minutes with Linda.

Linda told me that I would get paid a week of my current salary for every year I had spent at JWT. She was sorry it was not more, adding that she was sure I had saved something during all the good years.

Fat chance! I said to myself. *I have a house full of kids to educate!*

My mouth was dry. I couldn't talk.

"Okay," Linda said, rising. "It's not necessary for you to go back to the office to pack up. We'll handle that."

The "we" again. Linda was ready for prime-time.

"I want to have a going away lunch for you, Michael, you've contributed so much," Linda said, standing. "I will call you to set that up. And Jeffrey Tobin in Personnel will see you whenever you want to go over all the details of your severance package."

21

The thought passed through my mind of suing JWT, or writing nasty letters to all the clients. But Martin and Linda had already thought of that. "You will probably want to become a creative consultant of some kind," Linda continued, her tone more positive now, "and Martin and I would, of course, give you fabulous recommendations. I will personally help you in any way I can," she added. I was dead at JWT, but she was willing to keep me on some kind of life support, if I was a good boy.

Being fired is not the best way to start a consulting company. Yet I knew I needed the goodwill of JWT to have any chance of getting business from my old clients, or anyone else. If I caused trouble, I was trouble, and I'd never get any work.

The pesky waiter came up again, and I waved him off again.

Linda gave me a squeeze on both arms, almost — but not quite — a hug. "Be sure and call Jeffrey, Michael. He likes you. He will help you as well."

Then she turned quickly and strode out of the restaurant.

The waiter returned, one last time, and presented me with the bill.

Outside, the sun was shining. I suddenly, desperately realized I had nowhere to go.

For the first time in twenty-five years, I had no clients waiting for me to make sense of a communications campaign. I started walking and found myself crying on the street. It was humiliating. Crying! Me! Yet at fifty-three I had just been given a professional death notice. I knew in my heart it was going to be a bad time to be old and on the street.

And so it turned out.

Yes, I'd like a job. I hadn't said those words for thirty-five years. It had been thirty-five years since I had taken my entry-level job at JWT. And it had been ten years since I had been fired from my high-level position at JWT. I had set up my own consulting company, and I got a few good jobs right away from my old clients. Then, slowly but surely, fewer and fewer of my calls were returned. It had been months since my last project. Even a latte was becoming a luxury I could no longer afford.

Now, looking across my latte at this confident, smiling Starbucks employee, I felt sorry for myself. She seemed carefree to me, so young, so full of options. Later, I would learn that she had seen more hardship in her life than I could conceive of having seen in three lifetimes. Her mother, who died when she was just twelve, was a dope addict. She had never known a father. When her mother overdosed, she had been sent to live with an aunt, another single mother, who already had several of her own father-less children to care for. Her aunt was an aunt from hell. She would later tell me of the horrifying time she had fallen down the cement stairs of the project in Brooklyn where she lived. Her hip was broken, but her harried aunt just screamed at her for being so clumsy and refused to send her to a hospital. The bone set, but in a terrible way that guaranteed constant pain. Despite the confidence that she projected to me that day, she was even then in pain, physical and emotional.

But at that moment I was still at the center of my own universe, and my own problems were all-consuming.

To me, this young woman had great power — the power to employ me. *Yes, I would like a job.* As soon as the words had come out of my mouth, I was horrified. What was I do-ing? Yet, at the same time, I knew I wanted a job. I *needed* a job. And, I presumed, I would easily get a job at this Starbucks store . . . or would I?

The Starbucks employee arranged the papers in front of her, her smile dis-appeared, and she gave me a hard look. "So, you really want a job?" she said incredulously, shaking her head. She had clearly become more ambivalent about me as we got into the real possibility that I might work for her.

It suddenly struck me: *Her invitation to a job had been a kind of joke.* Maybe she had just decided to pass a few minutes making fun of me, the boring, uptight guy who seemed so full of himself. Maybe she had acted on a dare from another employee. But to her surprise, I had taken her up on her invitation.

She eyed me skeptically. "Would you be willing to work for *me?*"

I could not miss the challenge in her question: Would I, an old white man, be willing to work for a young black woman?

She later confided to me that her angry, bitter aunt had told her repeatedly as she was growing up, "White folks are the *enemy.*" From her point of view, she was taking a risk in even offering me a job. She was not willing to go an inch further until she was sure I would not give her any trouble.

I too was ambivalent. The whole situation seemed backward to me. In the world I came from, I should have been the one being kind enough, philanthropic enough to offer her a job, not the one supplicating for

25

the position. I knew that was a wrong senti-
ment to feel, terribly un-PC, but it was there
nonetheless, buzzing under the surface of
the situation. This young woman clearly
didn't care if I said yes or no to her job offer. How had she gotten to be such a win-
ner? My world had turned upside down.

New York City, 1945. My parents always
seemed to be going out to cocktail parties
and dinners. I was a lonely little boy. As
usual, they were not home when I returned
on the bus from Buckley School, but there
was Nana, as always, waiting for me with
arms outstretched and a big smile on her
face. I rushed into her commodious bosom.

This old woman who lived with us in our
imposing brownstone on East Seventy-
eighth Street was the love of my young life.
She was my family's cook and my closest
companion. I spent all of my time with her
in the warm and delicious-smelling basement kitchen, imitating Charlie Chaplin and
making her laugh. She gave me delicious
treats of nuts and raisins. When her father
in Virginia was sick, I told her that she
should go back to see him. Two weeks later,
her father died. Nana thought I was "sent
by God." She told me I would be a man of
God someday, a preacher. I had buckteeth
and big ears, but Nana said, "You are a

handsome boy." She told me I was going to be a real heartbreaker.

Later, I overheard my parents talking in the library. Their voices were low. I crept up to the door to hear them better.

"Nana is getting too old to climb the stairs," Mother said.

Our brownstone had four floors, with seventy-three steep stairs — I'd counted them many times to ease my boredom.

"Yes, I think it is all becoming too much for her," Father agreed.

My heart dropped with dread. *They must not let Nana go.* I ran to her, crying, but couldn't tell her what I'd heard.

Weeks later, when I came back one afternoon from school, Nana wasn't waiting for my bus. She was gone. Mother had hired a refugee from Latvia to be our cook. She was nineteen, and Mother told me she was doing a good deed in hiring her. The Latvian worked hard, but she barely spoke any English and didn't talk to me, or even look at me. And she was scared to go near me, or anyone else, which I learned much later was because the Nazis and the Communists had raped her.

But, as a young child, I only understood that Nana was gone, and I was alone again in the big house. The kitchen was cold and bare without her, yet I didn't want to leave the room where she had been. I sat quietly on the kitchen windowsill and watched the raindrops racing down the glass. I picked one raindrop to beat another to the bottom of the glass. If I picked the right one, I told myself, I deserved to have a wish come true. Then I wished that Nana would come back.

Less than a hundred yards from the brownstone I lived in from the ages of one to five, as I applied for a job at Starbucks, I was suddenly feeling the hole in my heart for a woman I hadn't seen for almost sixty years. Nana had been much older than the Starbucks employee facing me today. Nana was loving and large and soft. This young woman was professional, small, with a great figure. Nana had several gaps in her warm smile. This young woman's smile was a perfect, dazzling white. Nana was like a mother to me. This woman had already made clear she would relate to me as a boss to an employee.

There was really nothing these two women had in common — except they were both African-Americans. Like so many white people I knew, I appreciated the idea of integration, and yet, the older I got, the more it seemed that in my Waspy social circle, white people stuck with white people, black people with black people. For me to relate to an African-American woman on a personal, honest level opened memories of the only truly close relationship I had ever had with an African-American woman.

This young Starbucks employee did not realize that because of Nana, I was emotionally more than willing to work with her — I could not help but trust her. It was an irrational feeling, I told myself. How could a sixty-three-year-old man be influenced by an emotion from the heart of a four-year-old child — but there it was. *Would you be willing to work for me?* she had asked.

"I would *love* to work for you."

"Good. We need people. That's why we're having an Open House today, and I'm here to interview people for jobs as baristas." She barely looked at me as she told me these facts. It was as though she were reading me my Miranda rights instead of selling the job. "It's just a starting position, but there are great opportunities. I never even finished high school, and now I'm running a major business. Every manager gets to run their own store and hire the people they want."

She handed me a paper.

"Here is the application form. Now we will start a formal interview."

She reached out her hand.

"My name is Crystal."

The whole time, I had still been sitting with my latte and papers at my corner table. My briefcase on the table fell to the ground as I rose awkwardly partway out of my seat, shook her hand, and said, "My name is Mike."

I had called my business Michael Gates Gill & Friends because I was in love with the sonorous sounds of my full name. But here I felt that "Mike" was the better way to go. The only way to go.

"Mike," Crystal said, once again shuffling the papers at the table before her, still not looking at me, "all Partners at Starbucks go by their first names, and all get excellent benefits."

She handed me a large brochure.

"Look through this and you will see all the health benefits."

I grabbed the brochure eagerly. I hadn't realized the position offered health insurance. Rates had gotten too high for me to afford my health insurance, and I had let it go, a mistake that I had recently found out might have serious repercussions for me. Any remaining ambivalence I had about the job went out the window.

Just a week before I had had my annual physical with my doctor. Usually, he gave me a clean bill of health. But this time he shook his head slightly and said, "It is probably nothing, but I want you to have an MRI."

"Why?"

"I just want to make sure. You said you had a buzzing in your ear?"

"A *slight* buzzing," I hastily replied. I never gave Dr. Cohen any reason to suspect my ill health. I never even told him if I was feeling ill. He was a great practitioner of tough love — which meant that he was relentless in finding anything wrong with me.

"*Slight* buzzing. *Buzzing!*" he said in his usual, exasperated way. He was impatient with my artful dodging. "Get an MRI, and then go see Dr. Lalwani."

"Dr. Lalwani?" That did not sound encouraging.

"Michael, you are a snob," Dr. Cohen told me, "and that could kill you someday. Dr. Lalwani is a top ear doctor. He got his doctorate at Stanford. That make you happy?"

After a lifetime of treating me, Dr. Cohen knew me too well.

I had the MRI. Dr. Cohen had told me that it would only take a "few minutes."

I lay there for at least half an hour. And I also did not like the fact that I heard other

31

doctors come in and out of the room.

"What's going on?"

"Nothing," the young orderly told me. "We will send the MRI up to Dr. Lalwani. He wants to see you."

I was angry. Angry with Dr. Cohen for insisting on this stupid MRI. I had been healthy all my life. And I was not about to stop now. I could not afford any ill health.

Dr. Lalwani kept me waiting for most of the afternoon. I saw people go in and out of his office. Finally, Dr. Lalwani appeared, smiling from ear to ear. Was that a hopeful sign? Lalwani gestured me into his office. It was small and cramped and piled with papers. Not reassuring. I would have preferred a large corner office, with a comfortable couch. He was obviously not doing that well in his profession.

"Mr. Gill," he said.

"Michael," I told him, trying to be kind.

But he was insistent, smiling harder. "Mr. Gill, I have some bad news for you . . . but then you knew something must be wrong . . . am I correct?"

I knew something must be wrong? Was he crazy? I thought everything was all right.

"What are you saying?" I could barely contain my anxiety and my rage at his calm demeanor.

"You have a rare condition. Fortunately, it is in an area that is a specialty of mine."

"What is it?" I almost shouted, but Dr. Lalwani was not to be rushed.

"Something very, very rare." He smiled again. "Only one in ten million Americans."

I waited, filled with anger, but also with an animal sense I had to let the good doctor do it his way. I was already scared enough to yield to his academic style.

"You have what is called an acoustic neuroma. My specialty. But very rare. It is a small tumor on the base of your brain . . . that affects your hearing."

For a second I could not see or hear anything. It was as though I had been given a blow directly to my head and heart. I think I might have stopped breathing.

Dr. Lalwani, sensing my extreme distress, hurried on.

"This condition is not fatal," he said. "I can operate. But I must tell you the operation is very serious."

I recovered sight and sound just in time to hear those ominous words. "Serious" coming from a surgeon was not something I wanted to hear.

"What do you mean?"

"We bore into the skull, and it is an operation on the brain. Literally, I am a brain surgeon . . . this *is* brain surgery."

He was so confident in himself. I hated him for being so willing to operate.

"Your hearing may not be restored. The tumor is causing the buzzing. It will take one or two weeks before you can leave the hospital," he said.

"Before I can leave the hospital," I repeated numbly.

"And several months before you will be fully recovered. But the rate of recovery is very high. Fatalities are very rare. Only a few actually die."

A few . . . die? Was he mad?

"When do I have to have the operation?" I stammered out. My mouth was dry.

"I would do it right away . . . but you might wish to wait several months, come back, we will have another MRI, see if the tumor has grown. You might have a very slow-growing tumor."

Finally, a ray of hope. Like everyone, I hated the idea of hospitals. Friends had died in hospitals. Not to mention I was broke. Any postponement was a gift from God.

I got up quickly, shook his hand, left his office, and immediately called Dr. Cohen.

He was not reassuring.

"Sounds like you should have the operation," he told me.

"Yes," I said, faking agreement, "but I will wait a few months for another MRI."

I was buying time.

Giving up health insurance for myself was bad enough, but not to be able to afford health insurance for my children was much worse. I wondered if the tumor was in some karmic way a punishment for my behavior.

Now, sitting across from Crystal, I read the Starbucks brochure about the insurance benefits with particular interest. They seemed extensive, and even covered dental and hearing — something I had never been given as a senior executive at JWT.

I looked up at Crystal, hopeful, "Does this cover children?"

"How many kids do you have?"

"Five," I said, thinking about how I was used to saying "four." Five.

Crystal laughed. Then she smiled, almost kindly.

"You've been busy," she said.

"Yes."

I did not want to say any more; it was way too complicated to explain in a job interview.

"Well," she went on, still with a positive tone, "your five kids can *all* be covered for just one small added deduction."

What a relief. My youngest child, Jonathan, was the main reason I was so eager for work. It wasn't his fault. It was all my fault.

I had met Susan, Jonathan's mother, at the gym, where I had started to go shortly after I was fired. I needed a reason to get out of the house every day, and exercise became my new reason for getting up and out.

One morning I had been lying down on a mat resting. I was in a room that happened to be empty at the moment and was occasionally used for yoga classes. Susan had come in. It was clear she did not notice me and thought the room was empty. She was crying as she moved over to lean against the wall.

"Are you okay?" I asked. I was uncomfortable around emotional people.

She was startled, but did not stop crying.

"My brother is dying of cancer . . . just days to live . . ."

"That's tough," I said, sitting up on my blue mat, getting ready to leave.

"And just last year I lost my father to lung cancer."

"Tough," I repeated, standing up. I should have continued my progress out of the door, but I did not feel I could just leave her with her sorrow.

36

I moved closer to her.

"Don't worry," I said, not knowing where these words came from. "You will soon be happier than you ever have been before."

She looked up at me. Susan was small, barely more than five feet, with lots of dark hair and brown eyes. I am over six feet tall, with little hair and blue eyes. We were a study in contrasts, an odd couple for sure.

Susan rubbed her tears away, but more kept flowing.

"What?" she said, not quite believing that she had heard correctly.

I could not believe what I had said. Where had those crazy words come from?

But I repeated them.

"You will be happier than ever."

She nodded, as though understanding at some level.

I turned to go.

"I like a man who does yoga," she said. "It shows flexibility."

Susan and I started our relationship on totally false assumptions. She had taken me for someone interested in yoga. I had no interest in yoga. I did not like to stretch: It made me feel even more *inflexible.* I was rigid about many things. Physically. Mentally. Emotionally. I liked old songs, old ways. Until now, my past had worked well for me. Susan had no idea about what I was really like. Meeting me in the yoga room, she thought I was a flexible, perceptive person who could understand the deeper, more positive profundities of life. Like I was some wise guru.

It is funny, sometimes, how wrong people can be.

Susan was so wrong about me, and I was so wrong about Susan. I took her for a sad waif, a person who needed comfort and protection. Yet I learned later that she was an accomplished doctor of psychiatry with a large group of enthusiastic patients.

I thought she needed me.

She thought I could help her.

We were both so wrong.

Yet there was an immediate attraction between us. Was our powerful chemistry proof of the saying that opposites attract? Especially early morning in a gym. I had nothing better to do. And she had two hours free before she had to see her next patient.

Since I had been fired, I had found it impossible to make love to my wife, not that we tried that often. Like many married couples, we made love only occasionally. Still, it had scared me when I had tried to perform last time and failed. That physical failure compounded my recent professional failure. I had always counted on sex as a joyous release. Now it was one more sign of my seemingly irreversible decline.

Until I met Susan.

Yet, despite the attraction, I moved to the door. I *was* inflexible, and did not have affairs . . . especially with people I met at a less-than-exclusive gym.

"Would you like to have a cup of coffee?" Susan asked gently as I moved toward the exit. I almost did not hear her. She spoke so softly.

I found myself saying, "Sure, let's have a cup of coffee."

What could be the harm in having a cup of coffee with a sorrowful little person? We could get a latte at Starbucks and I could cheer her up.

But instead of Starbucks, she suggested her apartment. I went with her, and I was hooked. After that, I saw Susan almost every morning when she was free — which was two or three times a week.

Susan was not that young. In her mid-forties. She told me that her gynecologist had told her she could not have babies. So she said she saw no point in getting married.

"Marriage is for having kids," she said. "Sex is better without the bonds."

"Not to mention you already *are* married," she reminded me, glancing at my ring to confirm the fact.

I acknowledged her point with a significant amount of guilt. I loved how Susan made me feel, but I wanted to have my cake and eat it too. I loved my wife and wanted my four kids to live in a stable family environment.

Then one morning Susan called me at home — something she had never done before.

"I have to see you."

"When?" It was seven-thirty a.m. I had not even had breakfast.

"Now."

She was standing naked in her apartment; the curtains open to the East River. It was a March morning, but the sun was bouncing off the water.

"Michael," she whispered, "I'm pregnant. And God has told me I should have this baby."

My heart stopped. This was not on my agenda. I had lost my job and was struggling just to support my own family. I did not need another child.

"What are you thinking?" she asked.

"You have got to decide," I said.

"Tell me."

"No," I said, getting up. I was not going to tell her to have an abortion. This might be her only chance for a child.

"It's a miracle, Michael, but I need your support."

"I'm broke."

She laughed. Susan had another misapprehension: She thought because I dressed well and seemed well off that I was rich. She had no idea that behind my Ruling Class attitude I was getting poorer every day.

I had kept my relationship with Susan secret, but when Jonathan was born, I told my wife. She could not stand it.

"An affair is one thing," she said. "A child is another."

Betsy is very clearheaded.

"I just can't do it," she told me. "I'm not made for this kind of thing."

So we got an "amicable" divorce, although she was rightly furious with me for being so stupid.

"I thought we would spend the rest of our lives together," she said. I felt terrible.

My kids, now practically grown-ups, were understanding in a grown-up way, but hurt and angry too. I had given Betsy our big house, and she had enough family money to be okay, but I knew it wasn't just about

41

money. I had ruined her life.

And ruined my own life as well.

I took a small apartment in a New York City suburb. Desperately wanting to do the right thing after doing all the wrong things, I resolved to try to be there for Susan and my new child, Jonathan. I would come by around four or five a.m. and play with Jonathan so Susan could have a little sleep.

I was doing it out of a sense of obligation. But an unexpected thing happened. I became more and more attached to Jonathan. And he to me. Together, Jonathan and I would watch the dawn. When my other children were young, I did not have the time to watch them catch the wonder of each new moment. I was working twelve-hour days at JWT.

Here, I was being given another chance to be a father — in many ways, an opportunity I didn't deserve. I loved to see Jonathan grow before my eyes; to watch as he waved his little hand as though conducting when I would sing a gentle song, or hear him laugh with such uninhibited delight when I threw a stuffed animal up in the air.

One day, when I was putting my sleeping baby back in his crib, Jonathan opened his eyes and smiled at me. He opened his mouth and out came the beautiful sounds

"Da da." Two simple, heartbreaking syllables. Thinking back to how I had missed such magical moments with my other children caused a physical pain in my chest. And for what? For a company that rewarded my loyalty with a pink slip. I wanted to sit each of my children down and instruct them: *You only live one life; take it from me, live it wisely. Weigh your priorities.*

I spent less and less time chasing new clients, and more and more time with Jonathan. He loved me and he needed me. I was somebody wonderful in his eyes.

Jonathan seemed to be the only one who felt that way these days. Susan had gradually lost interest in me, first as a conversationalist. She told me I was "boring." I was not open to new ideas. And then she lost interest in me as a lover. She told me I was "too routine." In a peculiar way, the more available I became to her — after divorcing my wife, and having fewer clients and work to do, more time on my hands — the less appealing I was to her. She imagined me as a man at the top of America, fulfilled, productive, successful, and happy. She got to know me as I was: an insecure little boy not that good at dealing with reality.

Jonathan was my last fan, and my best pal. But now he had started spending his days

43

in school, so I was left with more time on my hands, fewer excuses for not finding work, and a greater need for a job just for bare survival. Hell, I wasn't even providing my little boy with health insurance.

How had I managed to be so incompetent in all of my personal and professional relationships? I tried to clear my mind of all my guilty, negative thoughts and focus on Crystal and this surprising interview. By luck or on a whim, Crystal had given me a chance — maybe my last chance — to stop my downward spiral. I did not want to blow it.

I looked up at Crystal and tried to give her a confident smile.

She wasn't buying it. It was clear that Crystal was balancing a personal dislike for me with her commitment to being a professional. Her store was in desperate need of new workers. And I was desperate for work. *Convince her,* I told myself. *Convince her that this is a match made in heaven.* I willed myself to be positive.

"Now I want to ask you some questions about your work experience," Crystal said in a cool professional tone.

I was suddenly very worried. After finding out about the health benefits that Starbucks offered, I really wanted this job. Was Crystal going to be another young woman like Linda White who would end up cutting off my balls? I didn't care, so long as she hired me.

"Have you ever worked in retail?"

Her question startled me.

I tried desperately to think. . . . *Quick, what is retail?*

"Like a Wal-Mart?" she helped. I sensed, for the first time in the interview, that Crystal might have decided to be on my side. This whole thing had started as a joke or a dare with her, but maybe, just maybe, she had come to see me as a person who really needed some help.

It suddenly struck me how much a life of entitlement had protected me from the reality everyone else knew so well. Maybe Crystal could help me get a grip, yet I could not even grab the saving rope she had tossed me in this job interview: I had never even been inside a Wal-Mart.

Crystal made a little mark on her paper and moved on. I felt very nervous. This was not going well.

"Have you ever dealt with customers in tough situations?" Crystal read the question from the form and then looked up at me. But her eyes were softer; now she seemed to be willing me to answer this question correctly.

Yet I was still at a loss. Was it tough to talk to the CEO of Ford? Yes, but that wasn't what was going to get me this job. I remembered that I had done advertising for Burger King and had worked at a store one morning to get a feeling for the business.

"I worked at Burger King," I said.

Crystal gave me a big smile.

"Good," she said. "And how did you handle a customer when things went bad?"

"I listened very carefully to what they were saying, then I tried to correct what was wrong, and then I asked them if I could do anything more." I spouted gibberish from some forgotten brochure I had written on how to handle bad situations.

Crystal smiled again and made a mark on the paper.

"Have you worked with lots of people under tough time pressures?" she asked.

"Yes," I said, keeping it vague. Working late on an advertising campaign for Christian Dior was different from serving lattes to hundreds of people on their way to work.

Crystal ticked down the list. "What do you know about Starbucks? Have you visited our stores?"

I was off and running. During my job

seeking over weeks and months, I had been in many Starbucks around New York. I leapt at the opportunity to show my knowledge. "The Starbucks stores in Grand Central are always busy, and *none* have seats, so I can't sit down, but the store on Fifth Avenue at Forty-fifth Street is really comfortable, and the one at the corner of Park Avenue has a great view, and —"

"Okay, Mike," she said, cutting me off, "I get it." She smiled. "Since you seem to be a fan, I think you'll like this question: And what is your favorite drink?"

Once again, I was able to be honestly enthusiastic. I love coffee in many forms, and Starbucks was my favorite place to get it.

"What's the difference between a latte and a cappuccino?" Crystal asked.

Here she had me. I liked both drinks, but did not know the difference. "I don't know. . . . The cappuccino has less milk or something?"

"You'll learn," she said, marking my form again, but I thought that response was positive. Just her saying "You'll learn" was a confidence builder for me. I had almost given up on the thought that I could learn or do anything new, or that anyone would invest the time in helping me learn a new job.

Crystal stood up. The interview was clearly over.

I stood up as well, almost knocking over my latte in my eagerness. We shook hands.

"Thanks, Crystal," I said, being as thankful as I ever had been in my life. She must have sensed the true gratitude behind my everyday words.

She laughed. What was so funny about what I had said? She was obviously now just getting a kick out of the whole situation. And me. Maybe I had shown her that the "enemy" was someone she could easily handle. Or, even better, maybe she had discovered that I was not just an old white man, but also a real person whom she could help. Whatever the reason, she seemed much more relaxed with me.

But then she got serious again. "The job is not easy, Mike."

"I know. But I will work hard for you. I promise you this."

She smiled, and maybe there was a little bit of pride in it. Later, I would learn the reason. Eight years earlier, when she had been on the street, she could never have conceived that in the future, she would have a Waspy guy, the proverbial "Man" himself, all dressed up in a two-thousand-dollar suit, begging her for a job.

Crystal must have recognized the sincerity in my willingness to cross over the bar — from drinking lattes to serving them up. But I realize now that she must have also seen that I still had much to learn, and many preconceptions to shed.

Despite this, she was willing to take a risk, cross over class, race, and gender lines, and consider me for the job.

"I will call you in a few days, Mike," she said, "and let you know."

2
REALITY SHOCK

"Imagine we are all the same. Imagine we agree about politics, religion and morality. Imagine we like the same types of music, art, food and coffee. Imagine we all look alike. Sound boring? Differences need not divide us. Embrace diversity. Dignity is everyone's human right."
— a quote from Bill Brummel, documentary filmmaker, published on the side of a cup of Starbucks Decaf Grande Cappuccino

April

Several agonizing weeks went by, and I heard nothing further from Crystal. Every moment I was consciously or unconsciously waiting anxiously for her to call. I continued going to the Starbucks store at Seventy-eighth and Lexington where we had met, hoping to catch sight of her, but she was never there.

I also kept calling potential clients for my

marketing business, but my voice mail remained empty. More than ever I needed a job, any job. When I had first met Crystal, I was not terribly serious about the idea of working at Starbucks. But over these last weeks, waiting for her call, without any other options surfacing to give me hope, I had realized that Starbucks offered me a way — perhaps the only way — to handle the costs of my upcoming brain tumor operation and support my young son and my other children. To support myself. I was facing the reality, in my old age, of literally not being able to support myself. I had left my former wife with our large house, was down to the last of my savings, and now I was facing the prospect that I might not be able to meet next month's rent. I was even more desperate than I had been just a couple of weeks ago. Whenever my phone rang, I found myself almost praying it was Crystal.

Had I done something wrong during the interview? I wondered. Said something wrong? Or was I just the wrong gender or race or age for Crystal to want to work with me?

As I sat willing the phone to ring, I thought back to casting sessions for the television commercials I had created over the last decades. I had not hesitated to eliminate people for any imperfection. If an actor's smile was too bright, or not bright enough, if a young lady had the wrong accent, that person was dismissed. When hiring, I chose the people who were like me, with backgrounds like mine. Now, as the days went by and Crystal still did not call, I had a sinking feeling that maybe Crystal operated in the same way: Do the easy thing, stay clear of anybody different.

"Diversity" is a big word these days. But few that I knew ever really moved beyond their own class or background — especially in hiring people they might have to work with every day. In corporate America, diversity was an abstract goal that everyone knew how to articulate, but few I had known actually practiced it. Rather, it was simply a word we discussed in a vague way when the government might be listening.

My only hope was that Crystal needed new employees enough — or was courageous enough — to give me a chance. Wasn't it ironic that I was hoping Crystal would be more merciful than I?

I forced myself to stop thinking about it. Then, one morning when I was in Grand Central Station, my cell phone rang.

"Mike?"

"Yes?" I answered with some suspicion. The person on the other end didn't sound like anyone I would know.

"It's Crystal."

My guarded attitude changed instantly.

"Oh, hi!" I said enthusiastically. "So good to hear from you!"

"Do you still want a job . . . ," she paused, and continued coolly, "working for me?" It was as though she were eager to hear a negative response and get on with her day. I imagined she had a list of potential new hires she was working through. And most of those on the list were probably easier for her to imagine working with than me.

"Yes, I do want to work with you," I almost yelled into my cell phone. "I am looking forward to working with you and your great team."

Calm down, Mike, I told myself. *Don't be overenthusiastic.* And why had I said "team"? Crystal had talked about "partners." I knew that every company had a vernacular that was important to reflect if you wanted to be treated well. I was already going crazy trying to fit in. *Take it easy,* I said to myself, *or you will blow this last chance.*

It didn't seem to matter — Crystal didn't

really seem to be listening. You know how you can be talking to someone on the phone and sense that they are pretending to listen to you while doing something they feel is more important? I felt that way that day with Crystal. For me, this phone call was of crucial importance. To her, it was just another chore in a hectic day.

The casual way in which she offered me the job was humiliating.

"Okay," she said. "Show up at my store at Ninety-third and Broadway at three-thirty p.m. tomorrow."

"Ninety-third and Broadway?" I echoed, surprised by the address.

"Yes." She sounded like she was instructing a three-year-old. "Ninety-third . . . and . . . Broadway, and don't be late."

I was confused. "But we met at Seventy-eighth and Lex."

"So?" She was almost threatening. "I met you there 'cause we had a hiring Open House going on. That's the way we do things at Starbucks."

Crystal had taken on a tone I knew well. I had used this corporate by-the-book attitude when dismissing people I did not want to deal with.

"At Starbucks," she continued, "we pick a store, have an Open House, and the managers who need people interview. But that doesn't mean that's the store you will work in. I'm the manager of the store at Ninety-third and Broadway." She paused, and added, "Do you have a problem with that?"

Once again, the threatening tone. Yes or no? She had other people to speak to and was eager to complete this call. I could sense she was not enjoying this job offer.

"No problem," I hastened to assure her. "I'll be there tomorrow, and on time."

I sounded — even to myself — like an old guy speaking like a new kid at school. How embarrassing!

"If you want to work, wear black pants, black shoes, and a white shirt. Okay?"

"Okay," I answered.

She hung up. She did not even say good-bye.

Shit! That little call made me feel really depressed. In the last few weeks, as the reality of my hard life grew clear to me, to keep depression from overwhelming me I grasped at straws — any signs that I might have a chance to maintain my position at the top of American society rather than drop so precipitously to the bottom rungs. Through these days of waiting for Crystal to call, the prospect of working at Starbucks humiliated me, but I told myself at least I'd be working in the neighborhood I had grown up in. A nice neighborhood. A location that would help me in my transition from a member of the Ruling Class to a member of the Serving Class. In the midst of my obvious, impossible-to-deny fall from financial and social heights, Seventy-eighth Street was a comforting place to be.

I had never even been to Ninety-third Street and Broadway — wherever the hell that was. My policy in New York City was never to go above East Ninetieth Street or below Grand Central. Now I was going to be working in what I envisioned could be a very dangerous neighborhood. It was certainly far from the Upper East Side, where I felt at home.

And I also didn't like Crystal's attitude toward me. She acted as though I were some *dummy.* I felt how unfair she was being. Then I remembered with remorse that I had treated a young African-American woman who had once worked for me at JWT with exactly the same kind of dismissive attitude. Jennifer Walsh was part of a big push we made in the 1970s to hire minorities. It was our token — and short-lived — effort at diversity.

Simply because she was part of this minority-hiring initiative, Jennifer was suspect to me. I was supposed to be her mentor. Yet, until that moment in Grand Central after talking to Crystal, I had never experienced what it was like to be so casually dissed because of *my* different background. I realized with a sinking heart how casually prejudiced of anyone different I had been in my reactions at JWT. At the agency, we liked the fact that most of us had gone to Ivy League schools. We thought we were the elite of the advertising business. We all approached the idea of hiring anyone who hadn't gone to the crème de la crème of universities as lowering the status of our club — and that included many in the minority-hiring initiative.

Jennifer was nice, but she had graduated from some minor junior college with a two-year degree, and I never took her career at JWT seriously. I had told her to read ads for several weeks, not even to try to write one. Then I had given her a newspaper ad to write for Ford. Her very first ad.

Jennifer came into my office. It was clear that she was scared, even petrified, as she approached my big desk. Which made me feel that she was wrong for JWT; we had to project self-confidence to our clients. I blamed Jennifer for being insecure in this new circumstance. When I read her draft of an ad, I noticed that she had copied a whole paragraph from some other Ford ad I had given her to read. This was a form of plagiarism that we really hated at JWT. Perhaps because we were called copywriters, we could not stand anyone who was accused of actually copying someone else's work. Jennifer had just committed an unpardonable corporate sin. At least as far as I saw it.

Thinking back, I realize that she might not have known that this was against policy, and I certainly didn't point it out to her then. I literally did not give her error a second thought. Her stupid mistake gave me the excuse I needed. I went to management and told them that Jennifer might make a great secretary someday, but she did not "have what it takes" to master the higher art of advertising. I had no time for her, or the idea of diversity.

I realized with a kind of horror now, recovering from Crystal's casual handling of a job opportunity that meant so much to me, how casually cruel I had been in "helping" Jennifer. I had been a classic hypocritical member of an old boys' club, congratulating myself for my belief in minority advancement in the abstract, while doing everything possible in the practical world of the workplace — which I controlled — to make such opportunity impossible. I had consciously or unconsciously derailed Jennifer's attempt to penetrate my little world just because she was an African-American without the education or experience that mattered to me.

Jennifer had been moved into some clerical job in Personnel, and had gone from my mind until this very moment. Now I felt terrible. I imagined Crystal thought I was some dumb old white guy whom she mistakenly offered a job. I wouldn't fit into her world or be a good match for her needs — just as I had felt about a young black American woman several decades ago.

I also kicked myself for not listening to my daughter Laura over many years. Laura had a beautiful halo of brown hair that echoed the sparkle of her hazel eyes, and I had a picture of her now shaking her head in angry frustration as I refused to "get it." She had devoted much time to trying to introduce me to a more realistic view of the world, and because I had been so insensitive, I had failed to listen to her. Laura had a dynamic, positive energy; she laughed easily but she also had a feeling for how unfair life could be and as she grew up had adopted African-American causes like affirmative action. She would sit across the table from me during dinner and toss her beautiful curls in frustration as we argued. I had dismissed Laura's feelings and ideas of how to help others less fortunate as "hopelessly naïve." I had been secure in my bubble of self-congratulation: convinced that my top job in advertising and my resulting affluence were my just reward for being a great, talented guy . . . not simply status and success virtually given to me by birth and fortunate color in a world ruled by "middle-aged white men of your generation," as Laura had once phrased it. Laura and I had a kind of running argument when she was growing up. It seemed like from the time she was about ten years old, she took my whole affluent lifestyle as an affront when so many people had so much less.

Even though she was now at college, she had not lost any of her sympathy for people less fortunate. She had actually cried when I had dropped her off at the picture-perfect campus I had picked for her.

"What's wrong?" I asked her. I had worked hard to get her into this particular college, even calling up a trustee I knew to put in a good word.

"This place has *no* diversity," she had said, struggling to express her frustration with me and my attitude of entitlement as she gestured at the all-white group of freshmen streaming into a fancy, newly built dorm she was to inhabit. "You still don't get it!"

Now I realized with a painful awareness how wrong I had been to try and stifle Laura's view of the "real world" as unfair to those not born in the right class with the right skin color who could afford the right higher education. I felt an actual pain in my heart at that moment, realizing with regret my arrogant assumption that God had created me and those like me to rule because we were worthier than other races of people. Now, finally, I was "getting it" as I faced a new reality of what the world could be like without inherited advantages.

But was my hard-won knowledge too late to change my fate?

Maybe there *was* bad Karma, I thought to myself. I certainly deserved it. But I was not about to turn down Crystal's offer — whatever her attitude.

I woke early the next day and realized with a shock that I was just weeks away from my sixty-fourth birthday. They say April is the cruelest month, and as I struggled into my black pants for my Starbucks job, I shook my head in disbelief that I was probably going to celebrate my birthday by working as a lowly coffee server.

I didn't know whether to laugh or cry at my feeling of trepidation as I hurried from my inexpensive apartment in suburbia and leapt on a train to Grand Central. Then I ran as fast as I could with the mass of people for the subway shuttle over to Times Square. Even though there would be another shuttle in a few minutes, we stampeded toward the one in front of us as though it were our last opportunity to go anywhere that day. I could not believe how fast the crowd moved — it seemed like we were in a hundred-yard dash for some Olympic event. Why rush? I hadn't commuted to a job for years, and back then I had taken a taxi or a company car as I moved up in the privileged hierarchy of JWT. I had never been one of the people who took subways. Yet now I had no time to doubt the sanity of the forward motion — I rushed along with everyone else.

From Times Square, I transferred from one crowded train to another that was heading up to Ninety-sixth Street. Squeezing in just as the door was closing, I found myself pressed against people I would never want to know; forced into a kind of primal physical proximity. All faces were unfriendly. *How did I get to this place in my life?* I thought to myself. Soon the doors opened, and I was forced out onto the dirty platform. I climbed the steep stairs to Ninety-third Street with a pumping heart, beginning to sweat, although it was a cold day in the beginning of April.

Emerging from the subway, I struggled against the wind and then actually staggered as I approached the Starbucks store at the corner of Broadway. Icy rain made the pavement slippery. I paused. Now that I was there, I was in no hurry to open that door.

As I stared at the Starbucks sign, the reality of my situation hit me with a sickening impact. I felt numb, standing on the icy pavement in the wrong part of town. My dream of rejoining a big international company to become rich and in control and happy once again had turned into a humiliating nightmare. Yes, I was going to join a big international company, but in reality as nothing better than a waiter with a fancy name. I would have the very visible public embarrassment of being Michael Gates Gill dressed as a waiter serving drinks to people who could have been my friends or clients. It was like the old days when the Pilgrims put sinners in the stocks in the public square as a visible example to others to watch their ways.

The Puritan minister Jonathan Edwards had said: "We all hang by a thread from the hand of an angry God." Maybe there was an angry Puritan God who had decided to punish me for all my sins. Over every minute of the past few years, I had felt the heavy weight of guilt for hurting so many I loved. My former wife, my children, and even those few friends I still had. My Puritan ancestors would be raging at me. Yes, I thought to myself, maybe there really was a vengeful God whom I had offended.

Yet I had to admit that my reality was more mundane, and sad. I could not pretend that I was living out some kind of mythical biblical journey. I was not a modern Job; I was looking for a job. And I had to face the brutal yet everyday fact that I was here because of my own financial mismanagement, my sexual needs that had led me to stray. I was not some special person singled out for justice by God. I was, and this really pained me to admit, not even that *unique.* It was hard, terribly hard, for me to give up my sense of a special place in the universe.

Now I was forced to see a new reality: What I was experiencing, as a guy too old to find work, was a reality for millions of aging Americans today who could not support themselves and were no longer wanted by the major corporations in our country. In this state of numbed anxiety, ambivalence, and forced humility, I opened the door to the Starbucks store.

Inside, all was heat, noise, and a kind of barely organized chaos. There was a line of customers almost reaching the door. Mothers with babies in arms and in prams. Businesspeople checking cell phones. Schoolkids lugging back-packs. College kids carrying computers. All impatient to be served their lattes.

As I looked behind the bar at the servers of the lattes, one of my worries was confirmed: Virtually all the Partners were African-American. There clearly was no diversity. This was not a complete surprise to me, because I had noticed in visiting various Starbucks locations since my interview with Crystal that very few white people worked at any of the New York stores.

For the first time in my life, I knew I would be a very visible member of a real minority. I would be working with people of a totally different background, education, age, and race.

And it was also clear from what was going on in the store that I would be working extremely hard. There were three Starbucks

Partners strenuously punching at the cash registers taking the money and speedily, loudly calling out the drinks to other people at the espresso bar. The people at the bar called back the drink names, while quickly, expertly making the drinks, juggling jugs of hot milk while pulling shots of espresso. In rapid-fire order, they then served them up to the customers with an emphatic "Enjoy!" that was almost a kind of manic shout. The customers themselves would reach in for their drinks with a fierce desire.

This coffee business clearly was not a casual one to anybody — on either side of the bar. There was a frantic pace and much focused noise, like being part of a race against time. I had never been good at sports, and this store had that athletic atmosphere of people operating with peak adrenaline. With all the calling and re-calling of drinks, it seemed that I might be auditioning for a role in a kind of noisy Italian opera.

Suddenly I was very worried. Not just about race or class or age. Now I had an even more basic concern. I had originally thought that a job at Starbucks might be *below* my abilities. But now I realized it might be *beyond* them. This job could be a real challenge for me — mentally, emotionally, and physically.

I had never been good at handling money — it was a major reason I needed a job so badly now. Math was a subject I had never mastered at school. I had vivid memories of many math teachers claiming, "But this is so easy," as they scratched out some equation on the blackboard. I hated those teachers for their superiority. Even the simplest additions and subtractions were a challenge for me. Now the reality of all that money changing hands so rapidly at the Starbucks registers terrified me.

I had lost hearing in one ear due to my brain tumor. Hearing the complicated drink orders could be a serious problem for me. I was also scared by the idea that I had to understand tricky orders and call them out correctly in a matter of split seconds. Languages had never been my skill. My French professor at Yale had said, "I will pass you on one condition: You never inflict your accent on anyone else in this university." Yet it was clear I was now expected to master the exotic language of Starbucks Speak.

In that first instant, I realized with humiliation that my new job might be a test I could easily fail. I had worn the black pants with a white shirt, no tie. I was feeling lonely and afraid. Then Crystal appeared in a swirl of positive energy.

"Let's share a cup of coffee," she said, guiding me over to a little table in the corner. "Sit here, I will bring you a sample."

Maybe this was just Crystal's public, professional attitude, but I was grateful for it. She seemed much friendlier than on the phone. Perhaps, I thought, she had come to terms with hiring me and did not hate herself or me for taking this chance.

Soon I was sitting down in a small corner with Crystal and sipping a delicious cup of Sumatra. "This is a coffee that is known as having an 'earthy' taste . . . but I call it dirty." Crystal laughed, and I laughed too. Today Crystal had her hair up under a Starbucks cap, making her look very sophisticated, even glamorous. Two bright diamond earrings caught the light.

Maybe it was the coffee, more likely it was Crystal's ability to put me at my ease, but I was feeling a lot better.

Still, I was a long way from being *comfortable.* Out of nowhere, I had a sudden image of myself in a long past life, basking in the comfort of family and friends on a dock on a lake in Connecticut. Now that image of laughing and lounging so comfortably beneath a warming sun seemed like several lifetimes ago. The lake I had grown up on was protected by thousands of acres of private forest. It kept out the reality of a harsher world and surrounded me with fun and privilege.

I remembered as a young boy throwing apples at the poet Ezra Pound. Jay Laughlin, Pound's publisher, owned the camp next door and had brought Pound down to the lake for the day. Pound sat like a kind of statue at the end of the dock. At one point he rolled up his suit pants and dangled his white legs into the water, still not speaking. His legs looked like the white underbelly of a frog. There was something about Pound's proud strangeness that got to my young cousins and me. We picked up some apples we had been eating and started throwing them at him, missing him but sending up water to splash against his dark, foreign clothes.

Ezra Pound did not move or speak. My father laughed and kind of encouraged us in our behavior. My father had written a bestselling book, *Here at The New Yorker,* about his years at the magazine. In the opening, he had stated his philosophy: "The first rule of life is to have a good time. There is no second rule." Having a good time for my father meant upsetting apple carts. He

69

had no love for Pound's politics and enjoyed the scene.

My father had won his place on this lake by marrying into my mother's family, who had vacationed there for a hundred years. My father brought new money, earned by his Irish immigrant father, into her *Mayflower* ancestry. At the lake there was a powerful combustion of gentle Wasp politeness meeting up with my father's purposefully provocative Celtic rebel style. With a kind of self-righteous abandon my father joyously spent the money *his* father had worked so hard to earn.

"It is better to spend your money while you are still alive," my father would declare, his black eyes flashing with a kind of devil-may-care enthusiasm, seeming to mock his own father's hard-won acquisition and those uptight Yankees around the lake who pinched every penny.

My father loved to speak, he loved to write, and he loved, above all, to be the center of attention at parties. "Everything happens at parties," he would say. So there was a constant party on our dock at this exclusive, rustic lake.

My father was a spendthrift with his time as with all his many talents. He gave himself away to so many that there was never enough time at home for *me*. Never enough time for one-on-one, for father and son. When I was grown, and I moved away from home, he invited me to his parties, and that is the only way we saw each other. When he died, my need to go to parties died as well.

Now I found myself sipping coffee with Crystal — worlds away from the parties during those summers on that exclusive lake — yet as I laughed with her, I could actually feel my heart become a little lighter and my spirits rise a bit. This reality surprised me. Maybe it was the caffeine in this powerful coffee. But I also had to admit that I felt at ease in this totally new scene — having coffee in a crowded, upbeat bar as a way of beginning a new job. It was all so bizarre and foreign, like Alice through the looking glass. Or Michael Gates Gill breaking through to another place and class to find it wasn't so scary after all. I was stepping out from my old status quo, and as a direct result, I felt better than I had in days. Or weeks. Or months.

It was crazy . . . but maybe, I hoped, there was a method in this madness.

Crystal's voice broke through my daydream. "Mike, it is important you learn the differences in these coffees." I no longer had the luxury of time for philosophical self-concern. The bell had rung. I was in the ring. It was time to get involved in minute-by-minute efforts rather than heavy contemplation. Keeping up with customers' orders was my new job. I had to give up spending so much time thinking about the past and what I had lost. It was going to be a big challenge just to keep up with the present.

I was about to discover that at Starbucks it was not about me — it was about *serving others.*

Crystal had a serious look on her face and launched into a lecture as though I were some eager student of coffee lore: "Sumatra coffee is from Indonesia; the Dutch brought it there hundreds of years ago, and it's part of a whole category of coffees we call 'bold.' "

"We" again, I noticed, thinking back to Linda White and her "we" when she had fired me. Crystal could do the same.

"This is the way we welcome all new Partners," Crystal explained, leaning forward toward me as though to confide a great personal secret. "We believe that coffee is our business. Starbucks *Coffee* is our name. So we welcome all new Partners with coffee sampling and coffee stories."

Crystal sat back with a smile, and I smiled back at her. Her face now seemed so positive and cheerful. Even her brown eyes, which could be so cold, now seemed to sparkle with a kind of happy interest. It had become clear to me as she talked that she was intelligent and even passionate. At least about the coffee business. And I felt that maybe — just maybe — Crystal really was going to give me a chance to prove myself.

As I sampled the rich Sumatra brew, I was beginning to feel that I could handle this part of the Starbucks business. I loved coffee; I loved learning about the history of things. I glanced over at the Partners behind the counter, all working hard yet seeming to have a great time. While they were all so young, and while there was not a white face in the bunch, maybe, I told myself, I should be, like the coffee I was drinking, part of the "bold" category.

Then the store door swung open. In stepped a scowling African-American guy, well over six feet tall with bulging muscles under a black T-shirt. He was wearing a do-rag wrapped tight around his head that, to my eyes, made him look like a modern pirate. He had a mustache and some sort of hair thing happening on his chin. He was the kind of person that in the past I had crossed the street to avoid.

Crystal called to him, "Hey, Kester, come

over and meet Mike."

Kester walked slowly over to our table. I noticed a bruise on his forehead. He reached out a big hand.

"Hi, Mike," he said with a low baritone. And then he smiled. His smile transformed his whole face. Immediately, I felt welcomed. In fact, he seemed much warmer than Crystal. Why? Was this because he was much more confident he could handle me? Old white guys definitely didn't bother him.

"Kester, where did you get that?" Crystal said, pointing at his forehead.

"Soccer."

"Soccer?"

"Yeah, some of my friends from Columbia got me into the game. . . . It turns out they think I'm pretty good. A natural." Kester laughed when he said that.

But Crystal quickly got back to the business at hand. Her face took on what I was coming to know as her hard, professional look. I got a sense Crystal always liked to be in control. "Mike is a new Partner," she explained to Kester, "and I was wondering if you could do me a favor. . . . Would you be willing to be his training coach?"

I was to learn that nobody at Starbucks ever *ordered* anyone to do anything. It was always: "Would you do me a favor?" or something similar.

"Sure," Kester replied, "I'll change and be right back."

After he left, Crystal told me, leaning forward in her confidential way, "Kester never smiled until he started working here. He was leader of a group of bad . . ." She stopped, seeming to be conscious of telling me too much. She leaned back, adjusting her hair. She had so many moods. Confiding. Confidential. Serious. Cheerful. Professional. Wary. Now she was wary again.

Kester returned, dressed in a green apron and black Starbucks cap, yet still looked pretty intimidating . . . until he smiled. Crystal got up and gave him her seat.

"I'll bring you two some more coffee."

Crystal returned with a cup of Verona for each of us and some espresso brownies. I was surprised by the enthusiastic way she served us. I had never served anything to any subordinate in all my years in corporate life. But Crystal seemed to be genuinely enjoying the experience. She and Starbucks seemed to have turned the traditional corporate hierarchy upside down.

She launched into a detailed description of Verona, telling us it was a "medium" blend of Latin American coffees, perfect with chocolate.

"But, then," Crystal explained, giving us both a big smile, "all coffees go well with chocolate; they're kissing cousins. You'll like the taste of Verona with this espresso brownie."

She left us to enjoy our coffee and brownies. It was as though we were guests in her home. It was certainly a totally different experience than any I had been expecting. The Verona coffee with the espresso brownies was a delicious combination — Crystal was right.

Then Crystal brought us a Colombian coffee with a slice of pound cake.

"This is in the 'mild' category," she said. "Can you taste the difference?"

"It sure seems lighter than Sumatra," I said.

"Right, 'lighter' is a good word, Mike," she said, as though she were a teacher congratulating an apt pupil. "Don't worry, you'll learn all about lots of different coffees here. By the way, you are going to be paid for the time you have been sitting here drinking coffee and having cake with Kester. Not bad for your first day on the job!"

Crystal left me with Kester. Though she had seemed so relaxed, I realized it might be just part of her management style. She was probably just putting a "new Partner"

— me — at my ease. I realized Crystal was hard to read, and that it would take me a long time to really get to know her. She didn't fit into any of my neat categories.

Ten years earlier, I couldn't have imagined being so frightened and so eager and so desperate for this young woman's approval.

And ten years ago, I couldn't have imagined having espresso brownies, cake, and cups of coffee with someone like the physically intimidating Kester.

"Here's how it works," Kester said matter-of-factly. "We call it training by sharing. It just means that we do things together. I learn from you by helping *you* learn." He picked up my cup in his and stood up. "Okay, now that you've had your coffee, I'll show you how to make it."

I followed him behind the bar.

Later, I came to know that Kester was the best "closer" at Starbucks. Closing the store late at night is one of the biggest management challenges because you have to be responsible for totaling up all the registers and making sure everything is perfectly stocked for the next day. Kester always made sure he got everything done on time and done right.

I didn't know any of this on my first day on the job. I also did not know that one late night, months later, Kester would save my life.

3
ONE WORD THAT
CHANGED MY LIFE

"The human catalysts for dreamers are the teachers and encouragers that dreamers encounter throughout their lives. So here's a special thanks to all of the teachers."
— a quote from Kevin Carroll, a Starbucks Guest, published on the side of a Decaf Venti Latte

May

I stood at the Bronxville station waiting for the 7:22 train to New York. I was not due to start my shift until 10:30 that morning — but I wanted to give myself *more* than enough time. The train from Bronxville to Grand Central took at least thirty minutes. The shuttle from Grand Central was another ten to twenty minutes to Times Square. From there I would jump on an express up to the West Ninety-sixth Station. I could then walk just a block or so to my store. I was anxious. I had not mastered the commuting routine and did not want to be late. I did not think I could afford any mistakes at my new job.

Waiting on the platform on that May morning, I had a chance to look around Bronxville. The little suburban village had changed a lot in the last few days as April showers heralded May flowers. Like in the movie *The Wizard of Oz*, the black-and-white winter had gone and the spring colors had arrived. There were now masses of bright red and white tulips everywhere — almost garish in their profusion. The forsythia was a burst of yellow. The trees had that first green tint that was like a soft mist against the brightening blue morning sky.

I sighed and then out of nowhere began to cry softly. The tears silently ran down my cheeks as I tried to suppress them. I did not want to draw attention to myself in that mass of energetic commuters. The men and women all seemed to be dressed in Brooks Brothers suits and were bubbling with a kind of self-congratulatory exuberance that I now found sickening.

I was jealous of them for their confidence about their lives.

I hated them for the ease with which they

seemed to face their commute.

I knew I was relatively invisible to them. Dressed in my black pants, shirt, and Starbucks hat, I looked like what I was — a working guy. Just another of those people who showed up at odd times to join the commuter rush — but were heading for service jobs too menial for the Masters of the Universe to notice.

I tried to brush the tears away, but they would not stop. Maybe it was an allergy from all the pollen now filling the air? But I knew it was not.

There was something so incongruous and sad about my standing on that platform waiting for a commuter train in my uniform so many decades after I first arrived in this exclusive town. My father had decided, after my mother had several more children (it seemed to me that my father was anxious for another son, that I was a real disappointment to him, and that was why he kept trying) that we had to leave the city.

My father chose a huge Victorian mansion in Bronxville because it was close to the city and a good public school. But Bronxville was not a happy place for me.

Every single day when I walked to school, a bully named Tony Douglas would leap out from behind a bush, push me down, and twist my arm until I cried. It was humiliating to cry at eight or nine, but I could not — eventually — resist. I knew crying was the only way to get him to stop. He really hurt me. He scared me. It was like he might break my arm. In the winter he would push my face down into the snow and rub it until I begged him for mercy. I *had* to beg to get away from him. Then he would leap up and run away laughing. I would slowly rise, in real pain, trying to gather up my books.

Not that I could read. That was another reason that I was so unhappy in Bronxville. When I got to school, I was in for more daily humiliation. Try as I might, I could not learn to read. I really tried. All my classmates learned. It was terrible to be sitting there in the midst of my classmates and not see what they could see and not be able to speak out loud the words that they could so proudly speak. The words in the books the teachers gave me to read seemed to be created in some secret code that I could not break. The sentences jumped before my eyes. I tried to will myself to break the code, but could only guess what those black lines meant.

How horrible it felt to me to be alone in this public proof of my stupidity, my obvious inability and misery.

My failure was impossible to ignore.

Miss Markham was the principal in the elementary school. She was a terrifying figure. Dressed in a black suit, she would march down the halls issuing commands in a deep voice.

I was brought to her attention.

She called my parents to come in and speak to her.

My mother was embarrassed; my father was clearly angry. I had ruined his day.

"Why couldn't she see us at some other time?" my father asked my mother. "It's right in the middle of my morning!"

For some reason Miss Markham took my side. Somehow, she had decided, despite all the signs to the contrary, that I would turn out all right. She also had insisted on including me in the "parents" conference.

"I never talk about children behind their backs," she explained.

Right in front of me, she told my parents, "Michael will read when *he* wants to. Stop badgering him."

I was dumbfounded by her attack on my parents. For she was clearly very cross with them. I had always been told how wonderful my parents were. She seemed to feel that I should be protected from them in some way.

Her apparently irrational faith was eventually justified, although reading came to me not through any act of concentration or panicky desire, but just gently, easily, one summer in the country when I was ten.

Every summer we would leave Bronxville for a small country town in the mountains of Connecticut. Mother was much happier there. She had gone to Norfolk for summers when she was young, and there were still many friends from her youth who summered there. Her best friend from childhood had a house just a few fields away, and her son became my best friend. We would ride our bikes down the old dirt roads and go for swims in the little lake.

Mother would get me out of bed early in the morning so I could see the dew sparkling in the sun.

"Elve's jewels," she would say, hugging me with delight. "Is there anything more beautiful in the world than a summer morning in Norfolk?"

Sometimes she would get me out of my bed at night after I was asleep and take my hand and lead me out to look up at the moon.

"Isn't it glorious?" she would say, a happy lilt in her voice.

But my happiest memory was sitting with

Mother on a steamer rug while she read to me. Across the field I could see a group of birch trees. Their leaves would flutter in the soft breeze. . . . One moment they would be green, and then silver in the bright sun of a late summer afternoon.

We lived in a little bungalow built by her father in the midst of a huge field and backed by an endless forest where no tree had been cut or even disturbed for more than a hundred years. Thousands of acres of forest had been set aside forever. That secluded woodland was a refuge for me. I would wander with a bow and arrow, telling myself I might shoot something (although I never did), and the silence of the old trees, the gentle pine and fern smell, would comfort me.

I also liked the country because I could spend some time with my father. In Bronxville he had enthusiastically renovated a thirty-five-room mansion, bragging, "This is the biggest house anyone in the family has ever owned."

He took the winnings from selling our brownstone on Seventy-eighth Street in Manhattan and poured it all into this huge house. There was an acre of tile roof to repair. He built a two-story library. I overheard him telling his friends, "I always wanted to have a private library with a ladder like this," demonstrating the ladder that could move along the bookcases to reach the highest volumes.

He had volumes of old *New Yorker* magazines there. I would climb up the ladder and take those volumes down. It was as though I were communing with my father, although he was almost never home. Despite his apparent pride in the house, he seemed always eager to get away, back to his city life. I never saw him come into the library and actually read a book, or even sit down. Once we moved to Bronxville, he spent less and less time with me or his family. He would leave early in the morning and come home after I had gone to sleep at night.

But I liked looking through the old *New Yorker*s — the cartoons, and even the way the print marched across the page. Although I could not understand what it meant, I caught a glimpse of something my father was proud to be part of.

One afternoon in the country, I came into the bungalow from wandering around in the woods. Mother was having a nap, and my sisters, who tended to do things all together, were visiting friends. I was by myself in the old living room. I pulled out an ancient book. Since this was a summer cottage, most of the books had been bought many decades ago and been left to grow musty and damp on the shelves.

I took down a book that was very thick but had photographs. I opened a page to a photograph.

"General Grant," I read. I could actually *read* his name. I could read! First a few words and then more and more. Suddenly, the black print made sense in my brain.

I did not say anything to anybody, but by the time we returned to Bronxville that fall, I had learned to read many words. I was even confident enough to read in school.

Despite the fact I was by now in the sixth grade and was finally achieving what my classmates had accomplished years ago, Miss Markham was terribly pleased. I had justified her "crazy" faith in me.

One afternoon just before the end of that year, Miss Markham asked me to come to her home. When I finished sixth grade, I would be moving on to seventh grade in the same big brick building. But next year I would be part of "Junior High" and would be leaving "her school," where Miss Markham so clearly ruled.

She lived with another woman in a large house by the school.

She served me tea.

Then she took out a note she had written. She showed it to me. Her handwriting was very big and bold.

"Read it," she instructed with her bold voice.

"Michael Gates Gill is destined to be great," I read.

I looked up. Was this a test? Had I passed a reading test of some kind?

"Is there any more?" I asked, eager to read more to her. Without her, I might have had to go away to some school for "special students," as my parents had once discussed.

"No more to read," Miss Markham said, reaching forward and holding my hands in hers.

I noticed she had big eyebrows, and very bright brown eyes.

"I have made a decision," she said. "You, Michael," she continued, as though making a formal, public statement, "are destined for *greatness*. I don't care what you do, or what you don't do. I don't care if you go to some prestigious college, or don't go. I just know: You *are* great."

She sat back, dropping my hands, smiling at me.

I did not know what to say. I really didn't understand her point.

She leaned forward and spoke again. "I almost never do this," she said, "but once every few years I see some young person I feel has exceptional qualities. I want you to know that you are worthy. *You.* Not just what you *do.*"

Worthy? I thought, but what did that mean?

"Maybe you won't know what this note means now," she said, intuiting my hesitation and mystification, "but keep it in a drawer somewhere. Take it out once a year and read it. Now that you can read!"

She laughed, and then became serious again. I was just a small boy, and she knew she had not gotten through to me.

"You didn't think you could ever learn to read, did you?" she asked me in a softer voice.

"No," I said.

"But I knew," she said. "And I know that you are great. But you don't, do you?"

"No."

"Well, just remember I told you so."

I still just stared.

I had never known anyone who had gone to Miss Markham's house, or even talked to her as a person. Maybe that's why I was so shy now. Although I was shy with everyone. I knew she wanted me to talk, to say something in response to what she had given me. It was clearly a great gift. I sensed her love and support. But I didn't know what to say.

"My older brother," she said, uncharacteristically quietly, "was an alcoholic. Yet he had many wonderful qualities. I was not able to help him. I think, looking back, that he never knew he was wonderful."

Were there tears in her eyes?

"Keep the note," she said, her voice thick with emotion. "Just keep it."

She rose and walked me to the door, once again the Miss Markham of energetic forward motion and dynamic action that I knew.

We shook hands almost formally.

I left, and for some reason stopped at the corner and looked back.

She was watching me.

She waved.

I waved back.

I kept Miss Markham's words for several years, but then lost them when I went away to college and Mother threw out a lot of my old stuff. But I remembered that afternoon vividly, and still do.

I saw her once after I got out of college, at the Department of Motor Vehicles where we both happened to be renewing our licenses.

She had retired, and grown old. Her hair was white.

"Michael," she called to me, across the stale government space of the waiting room.

Her voice was the same.

I rose to meet her.

She came up to me.

"How are you doing?"

"Good," I said. "I went to Yale."

"You didn't have to go to *any* college," she said. "Remember my note to you?"

"Yes."

"And so do I!" she said, and left with a smile. "It's not what you do, it's who you are. And you are great."

My name was called at that moment, and I went up to the counter to complete the forms and get my picture, and when I was through, she was gone. I never made any more effort to see Miss Markham.

Even in my twenties at the DMV, I was still not certain how to respond to her belief in me. I had no words for her. But uplifted by her confidence in me, I had fallen in love with words.

Miss Markham might well have expected what happened. After I learned to read, I developed a passion for books. I discovered the world that words could bring to me. Starting when I was ten, I read for hours every day. I loved to escape into that world of words and books.

For life was still very lonely for me. My father would visit for weekends during the summer, but during the winter he was too busy to do things with me.

I had a few friends, but there was something horrible about this elite suburban town for me. In New York City, even when Nana left and I felt alone, I could still look out the window of our home at a wide range of people passing on the sidewalk outside. Old people. Kids. Policemen walking. Teenagers running down our block.

In Bronxville, in our huge house, there was no one even walking by . . . just the sight through our high hedge of a car with a squeal of tires turning a corner.

I fared better in the country. In Norfolk, there would be weekends when my father would let me caddy for him when he played golf. And he went to the lake with the family and I could spend a whole day in his company.

He would call out an invitation to Jay Laughlin, a man who owned the camp next door, when he was swimming by, "Get out of those wet trunks and into a dry martini."

Jay was, like my father, deeply engaged in the literary life as founder of the New Directions publishing company. But, unlike my father, he was very melancholy and could barely smile. Except in my father's presence, when Jay would laugh out loud.

Soon my father would have a group laughing at his jokes, and I could bask in his presence and the joyous atmosphere he created. It seemed to me that my father was the funniest man in the world when he was with grown-ups.

With me, he was awkward, but loving in his way.

Sometimes he would sing me songs sung to him by *his* father. "The Minstrel Boy." "Danny Boy." Old Irish tunes. At other times, during family meals, when he grew bored, he would recite poetry to us. Sad poetry. "Nothing to look backward to with pride," he would intone from Robert Frost's "The Death of the Hired Man." "Isn't that a sad summation of a life?" he would ask, addressing the whole table, but I would be quiet.

As a young boy I really had no idea what he was talking about.

Even later, at Yale, when I met Robert Frost, I failed to understand the sadness beneath his poetry. Of course, Robert Frost presented himself as a kind of jolly country gentleman. I remember running from a last class to a sherry party in honor of this famous poet. I did not have to change my clothes. I was, like all undergraduates in those days, wearing a jacket and tie. Yale had yet to experience the crashing wave of the Vietnam War and the joyous change to coeducation. We were still encased in a kind of carefully preserved amber of an ancient ambience in which Dink Stover and other well-dressed Yale heroes from decades ago were still very much alive. (Dink Stover was the main character of a bestselling fictional book of that name that was published at the very beginning of the twentieth century and is still in print today. Dink was a superlative athlete, but also very courteous. Above all, Dink Stover conducted himself like a true "gentleman." The climax of the book was when Dink's inherent greatness of character was recognized when he was tapped by Skull & Bones.) My professors addressed me as "Mr. Gill," and my English professor had invited me to "have a glass of sherry with Robert Frost."

Professor Waite greeted me at the door and ushered me in. There were already a half dozen other undergraduates gathered around a large man standing in the center of the room. Frost wore a thick tweed jacket and had a shock of white hair that seemed to have, through some magical means, been windblown despite the fact we were inside an overheated faculty lounge.

He greeted me with a strong grip and laughing eyes.

None of us asked him any questions about his "work." It would not have been polite in that social context, a little like asking a doctor to do a diagnosis when you were talking to him at a cocktail party.

In fact, I never remember discussing poetry and writing itself with *any* poet I met at Yale. Having a drink with W. H. Auden at Mory's, we wound up discussing the proper way to make a particular drink. When I was invited to meet T. S. Eliot, who had come to New Haven to give a lecture one evening, I was specifically told by my professor, Norman Holmes Pearson, "Don't ask him *any* questions. Rumor has it that he is dying of cancer and is on a lecture tour to try to raise money for his wife."

When Donald Hall, the current poet laureate, visited New Haven, I was asked to take him out to dinner. We ended up spending a wild night with many drunken undergraduates — which he seemed to find quite a relief. Once again, the subject of his poetry, or *any* poetry, never came up.

Part of the social obligation at Yale, as it

had been in my home life, was not to ask too many direct questions.

So as a young boy growing up, I would never have thought to ask my father what he meant when he quoted Frost, or any other poet. I was a receptive audience, and not encouraged to be more.

Almost every day my father would say, "Stay with me beauty for the fire is dying."

I asked him once what that meant.

"It's a line from a poem" was all he would say. I didn't truly realize until my father died what horrors he was really living with. Although there were some intimations of the tragedy he had endured.

On my seventh birthday, when Mother had a party for me after school, with balloons and cake, and even extra presents for my friends, my father happened to come home early and saw us all gathered laughing in the dining room.

He came into the room, and all of us fell silent. My father had a powerful presence, with great dark eyes, and he appeared upset.

He seemed about to speak.

"Yes, dear?" my mother said. She was always so anxious to get him to join in family activities. "We are just having a little party for Gatesy's seventh birthday."

"My mother died when I was seven," my

father said, and then he left the room.

My mother followed him out.

I don't remember what my friends and I said then, but I think we just got back to playing with all the presents Mother had bought.

But it was clear that my father did not feel comfortable talking with me or even just being with me.

I overheard him telling Mother once, "I can't wait until Michael Gates grows up, and I can have a decent conversation with him."

Yet — despite his clear discomfiture with me and my mother — my father was more a part of the family during weekends in the country than he ever was in Bronxville.

And when my father was away from us "working hard in the city" during the summer weekdays, I could swim and walk in the woods, and smell the pines and taste the amazing, fresh Norfolk air — full of the scents of field and forest — at night when I fell asleep.

And every night as I fell asleep I would smile, thinking that maybe Mother would come to wake me and take me to "her moon."

But Bronxville had no such charms for me.

How had I ended up here . . . standing at the Bronxville railroad station . . . living in a tiny apartment rather than a huge mansion . . . without family or friends? I brushed more tears away.

Once I got the job at Starbucks, I had tried to find an apartment near my store in New York City and discovered there was no way I could afford one.

I started to look outside Manhattan. Moving up to the upper reaches of the Upper West Side, out to the Bronx, Mount Vernon, and I even began to think of going as far as Brewster. There didn't seem to be anything I could afford closer to the city.

One day, I stopped during my apartment search in Bronxville to have a hamburger at a restaurant owned by an old high school friend. Phil told me he had kept his parents' house and had a small attic apartment on the third floor.

"The house is right by the railroad tracks," Phil told me, "but it's really convenient and I'll give it to you at a good price."

I jumped at the chance. The little apartment suited me. I liked climbing the old stairs and living in an attic of an old house.

The train arrived.

I got on, shuffling behind the herd of eager beavers. I knew that being morose was no way to start the day, and so I tried to recall *happy* memories about Bronxville.

My father would have great parties at our Bronxville home several times a year. He would always make a point of introducing me to someone I might enjoy. When I was young, he had me meet E. B. White because I had so loved *Stuart Little*. E. B. White was diminutive, kind, and curious. Just like Stuart Little.

Then, when I was older, he invited Brendan Behan, the wild Irish playwright, out to the house so I could meet him. I loved Behan for his crazy song that the bells of hell might go "ting-a-ling-a-ling for you but not for me."

I told myself now that I had had happy times in Bronxville. But I had to admit that those big parties, and these literary celebrities, really meant very little to me. I would have preferred more time alone with my father.

At sixty-four, I reminded myself, I would be dead soon . . . not just singing Behan's song. Did I want to spend the rest of my life mourning my past? It was time for a more positive approach to the few years I had left.

For some reason I thought at that moment, trying to squeeze anonymously into my seat on my way to my new Starbucks job, of F. Scott Fitzgerald's comment, "There are no second acts in American lives."

Was I on some hopeless quest to start a new life? Wasn't this commuting life I had now, something I had thought I so looked down upon, a sign that I was on the wrong track?

I took a deep breath, straightened up in my seat, and tried to think it through.

I felt that I really liked working with Crystal. It was hard to admit, but in many ways I really enjoyed working at Starbucks more than I had at my high status job at J. Walter Thompson.

Be honest, Mike, I thought, calling myself by my new Starbucks name. *You feel good about what you are doing. Just because you are wearing a green apron rather than a Brooks Brothers suit doesn't mean you can't enjoy it!*

I actually laughed out loud.

That happy sound made the commuters look at me.

They had not even noticed my tears, but laughter to them was clearly out of place.

By the time we got to Grand Central, I actually felt good. I rushed off the train, try-ing to get ahead of these upwardly mobile

Bronxville strivers. Few, maybe none, would be heading with me to Times Square and the Upper West Side.

As I squeezed into the shuttle, I stood taller.

There is nothing wrong with working at Starbucks, I told myself, *and a lot right.* I would be able to afford my little apartment. It wasn't the huge mansion I had occupied, or even the beautiful old New England farmhouse I had lived in with my former wife and kids, but it was now home to me. A room of my own.

The express train took me up to Ninety-sixth Street.

I climbed up the steep subway stairs into . . . sunlight. It was a beautiful day in New York . . . one of those rare spring days when there is an actual sparkle in the air.

I saw the green Starbucks sign on the corner of Ninety-third and headed toward it with growing optimism.

Another Fitzgerald quote came into my mind. Something he had written to his daughter after his wife died in a fire in a mental hospital in Asheville, North Carolina, after years of decline. Zelda had never fulfilled her early promise, and Fitzgerald wrote, "She realized too late that work was dignity."

Work is dignity, I repeated to myself. *That could be* my *mantra.*

Why had it taken me so long to realize this essential truth? Fitzgerald had written his daughter this key perception, yet I had fought my daughter Elizabeth, whom I called "Bis," when she had wanted to go to work. When she was just twelve years old, she had been offered a summer job helping the tennis pro with scheduling and teaching and I had turned down the job offer — without even talking to Bis about it.

"How could you do that, Daddy?" Bis had cried, tears cascading from her eyes.

"But I want you to have a chance just to *enjoy* yourself this summer."

"But I *like* to work," Bis had angrily replied.

For me, work was something one had to do, not what one should do. I admired those who never had to work . . . and lusted after the huge trust funds of some of my richer friends. I thought I was doing Bis a favor by protecting her from having to work. How wrong I had been.

Bis had always loved to work and be active in the world outside our home. Even when she young, she had loved to go to school. Since she was my first child, I did not realize how rare that attitude was. And even before her first day of school, Bis had taught herself to read. One day when I was reading in my favorite armchair, Bis climbed up into my lap and started to read the sentences of a Dick Francis mystery that I was engrossed with. She was only three years old at the time and I was amazed! How had she learned to read? Had she taught herself? Then I had an idea: Bis had learned to read by watching *Sesame Street*. The show had taught her. Of course, I found out later, when my other children came along, that it wasn't *Sesame Street* that had taught Bis — she had simply been born with an extraordinary facility for reading, which she had definitely not inherited from me.

Bis was also fortunate in that she was beautiful. Even when she a little girl, when I walked with her through the streets of New York, overeager photographers would sometimes stop me and ask to take her picture. A friend put her in a movie because he said he she was a "showstopper." Bis had a halo of blond hair and large blue-green eyes. But it was her brains and her general love of getting things done — working hard — that was really remarkable. After high school and college she went on to NYU Film School and then got a job as a gopher for Martin

Scorsese . . . not an easy boss. Then she went on to work for Harvey and Bob Weinstein — an even bigger challenge. But Bis seemed to love all the hard work they gave her. And her hard work was rewarded. She worked to help promote the movie *The Crying Game.* The producer was so impressed with her, he offered her a job directing a feature film. This was Bis's dream — to be a director. Even while working for Sorsese and Miramax, she had found time to make several short films. Now she would have a chance to direct a full-length feature. The movie, *Gold in the Streets,* was shot in New York and Ireland. Bis discovered that Ireland was a more open market for female film directors, and she moved there to continue her work.

Working hard had always come naturally to Bis. . . . Why hadn't I profited by her example? Her attitude should have taught me about the dignity of work — even as a lowly coffee-getting gopher, Bis had approached her jobs with true enthusiasm. I realized now what a miracle Bis was — she had not only reversed my reading disability but had somehow reversed my sense of work as a chore rather than a calling.

The thoughts of Bis comforted me as I opened the door and headed toward the back of my Starbucks store looking forward to more hard *work*.

I was hoping Crystal would be there and would give me something to do that did not involve the dreaded cash register. As anxious as I was to prove myself as a new Partner at Starbucks, I hesitated each day in going out front with the other Partners to deal with customers. I had yet to handle a cash register, and the thought terrified me. So I usually just stood there in the neutral zone of Crystal's "office." It was a little space with a desk, a chair, and a computer. In the last few weeks Crystal had usually turned to me after I had hung around for a while and asked, "How do you feel about cleaning today?"

I always responded, "I would like nothing better!"

Cleaning, I thought, would keep me from those terrifying registers. I expected to fail, and fail spectacularly, when I was forced to make change and make conversation at the same time, so I wanted to win Crystal's respect and build up her need for me in her store, in some area I could learn how to do.

Of course, I had absolutely no previous experience in cleaning. At home, my former wife had handled the cleaning chores, or had cleaning ladies come by to do the hard stuff like the bathroom and kitchen. And when I had been a senior executive, I never had to clean up my office area. Ladies armed with plastic garbage bags and vacuums would arrive late at night, sometimes as I was leaving. I prided myself on always being polite, but really gave little thought to how they made the whole space so clean.

"This is grout," Crystal said on my first cleaning duty day. "It takes a lot of work to get it out. We have tiles, and we have a grout problem. Or maybe I should say that we have a grout *opportunity.*"

It certainly was an opportunity for me.

Crystal gave me a special grout brush. Then she showed me how to fill up the mop bucket with hot water and a cleaning solution. I would sweep, then I would mop, then dig out the grout with the brush, then mop again. Just to do a few feet took many minutes. Hours to do the whole store. I attacked my cleaning job with a kind of manic energy.

Once Crystal came by and actually laughed at me.

"Mike, I have never seen anyone clean with such enthusiasm."

"I love it," I said, meaning it. I could see I was making a difference. Even the other Partners quietly gave me some respect. I guess they hadn't expected this old white guy to enjoy digging out grout so much.

Kester came by once and said with his engaging smile, "Watch out for the bathroom."

Sure enough, that very day Crystal said, "Mike, I am going to show you how to really clean a bathroom. You know how sometimes a car wash will say they are 'detailing' your car? We are going to 'detail' a bathroom. We'll do it together — once. Then I want *you* to make sure the bathroom is always sparkling."

Crystal made me put on gloves and had given me super-powerful detergent. I found myself down in and under the toilet bowl digging out all kinds of shit. I was surprised how little revulsion I felt for a job I would have previously thought too far beneath me and much too humiliating to even contemplate. But since Crystal seemed to be so positive about it, her respect for the challenge of cleaning a bathroom made me feel differently. It was a worthy effort to her, and who was I to argue with Crystal's view of work and the world? I also felt a surge of primal adrenaline based on my animal instinct that if I could succeed in doing something for Crystal, I could keep my job — whatever other difficulties I might encounter with the register or other challenges of this fast-moving retail environment. So I was more than happy to go with her mood of upbeat determination to do a great job of cleaning a toilet.

Soon the toilet was, indeed, sparkling.

She smiled.

"Mike, I've got to say I've never seen anyone clean like you."

She did not know I was betting my whole future at Starbucks on getting good at some job nobody else wanted. That way, I figured she couldn't fire me. That was how scared I was that I would lose this job. I didn't want to fail at what I now thought might be my last chance. The average age of the Partners in the store was about twenty. I knew I wasn't getting any younger, and it had been a fluke that I had this chance.

Yet I found my advanced age did not make me any more merciful to the old or needy. Understanding and adapting my behavior to the Starbucks experience was not easy. Especially at first.

One afternoon, I had just finished "detailing" the bathroom, and it was sparkling. I saw an old African-American man who was clearly a homeless person heading for the bathroom. I intercepted him and explained that it was closed for cleaning — a lie I made up because I was afraid of the mess he might make.

Crystal overheard me and gestured for me to follow her back to her office — never a good sign. I had learned that she never criticized anybody in front of the Guests, or even other Partners. She would take you aside — one-on-one — in her office.

"Mike, never refuse the bathroom to anyone," she said in a low, angry voice.

"But that old guy wasn't a customer, he couldn't afford —"

"He might not be a customer, but everyone who walks in that door is a *Guest.* That's what makes Starbucks different from anyplace else in New York. Haven't you noticed there are no public bathrooms in this city?"

For some reason, perhaps because I had just worked so hard to clean up such filth, I argued with her.

"But it's not Starbucks's job to provide toilets for the homeless."

Crystal did not say anything . . . for about thirty seconds. I could see she was furious. Her eyes seemed to enlarge with rage.

I shut up. Somehow, I had tripped over a land mine of emotion. I felt terrible, and scared.

"Look." Her words were spaced; I could

tell she was fighting herself not to yell at me. "In my store, in *our* store, we are . . . *welcoming.* Don't refuse that toilet to anyone, especially someone who really needs some welcome and not another person putting them down."

She had not said "not another white person" putting them down, but I read into it that way. But maybe I was being too sensitive. I *understood* that I had made a big mistake. Crystal, and Starbucks, didn't treat people like that.

I went back out front to try to find the guy, but he had gone. My rejection probably meant nothing to him — New York is an unfriendly city to someone trying to use a restroom. But I learned a valuable lesson that day. My old arrogance had come back as soon as I thought I had done a great job. How sad!

The next day, Crystal didn't even mention the incident. I was to learn that Crystal didn't harbor grudges. She let you know when she didn't like something you did, the moment you did it. And she never brought it up again.

"Now we move outside," she instructed. She had me wash down the sidewalk and all the windows and window ledges.

A week later, she pulled me aside. "I have

decided to make you my cleaning supervisor," she declared. "Sometimes I will have other Partners help you, and you can supervise."

I was elated. Promoted! I had been programmed at J. Walter Thompson to be excited by promotions. Moving from a copywriter to a creative director and then to a vice president and finally executive vice president and a creative director had been a series of great occasions. There was always a raise, praise in a congratulatory memo, a celebratory dinner at a fancy restaurant, and increased prestige with my peers. But then I realized with a powerful jolt that I was no longer in that world where such things really meant something. *This isn't some huge corporate hierarchy where it matters what title you have. . . . You're* cleaning bathrooms, *for God's sake!* I thought, laughing at myself . . . something I had never learned to do before.

Now, standing awkwardly in Crystal's tiny office space, I hoped to do more cleaning today. One more day away from those dreaded cash registers.

"Hey, Mike," Kester said, brushing by, "how are you doing?"

"Good," I said, "I hope to do some more cleaning today."

"No shit," Kester said, then we both broke

into laughter at his unintentional reference to toilets.

Crystal swiveled in her chair in front of the computer to face us.

"No street talk in here," she said, clearly not amused. Kester gave me a wink and continued on out front.

Crystal looked at me pointedly, the way a mother looks at her child who is acting out.

"He was just joking," I stupidly said. Kester needed no defense from me. And Crystal was upset. Why hadn't I just shut up?

"Mike, let me explain something to you," Crystal said, pushing her chair back.

She pointed to the wall behind me that had a paper taped to it.

"That's a paper with our uncompromising principles on it. . . . Read me the first one."

Crystal sounded like an angry teacher. Well, I would show her. Now I could *read!* I read out the first "uncompromising principle" with great power, force, and confident clarity: "To create a great work environment and treat each other with respect and dignity."

Crystal stood up. Even though I had read Starbucks's first uncompromising principle with such vigor, she still seemed upset about something.

"Respect," she said, reaching past my face to point at that word. "I don't think it's respectful to use street talk in here."

Her hand dropped. Her voice lowered.

"Mike, I don't mean to go off on you like this. *That's* not respectful!" She smiled. Crystal seemed to be regaining her composure.

"It's just that," she said, slowly, dragging out each word, "before I came here, I wasn't treated with respect by anybody . . . anytime. I never even heard that word. My mother was a dope addict. She died when I was twelve. I was handed off to an aunt who already had two kids of her own." Crystal threw up her hand in exaggeration. "Respect? In that crazy house? I don't blame her now, I can see where she was coming from, but then it really hurt me that my aunt didn't want me. She sure didn't treat me with *any* respect. My aunt hated me. She hated white people."

Crystal looked at me as though to say, *Now do you get it?*

"She called white people the 'enemy.' " It was as though Crystal was trying to shock me with her revelations of how disrespectful some people could be.

I was shocked. I was silent.

113

"My aunt did not treat me like an enemy, but she just made me feel like some unwelcome stranger in her house. Since I have been here at Starbucks I have been . . . welcomed."

Crystal turned and sat back down, once again the relaxed manager of her store.

"I'm sorry," I said.

"Don't be sorry, Mike. This respect thing might be new to you too." She laughed. "I've been here for years, and it's still new to me. You don't learn it overnight. I'm still learning. I just wanted to explain to you why it's such a big thing with me."

"Yeah, I notice that people at Starbucks seem more polite."

I had noticed that even from the first day I stepped through the door at Starbucks, I had also been treated with respect. When asking me to do something Crystal or my other Partners would always say, "Mike, could you do me a favor?" There was never an order given. I also realized that I had gained some self-respect by handling the cleaning and some of the tougher parts of the job. But Crystal didn't feel I had quite gotten the respect idea yet.

"The Partners are a lot more than *polite*," Crystal said, reacting to the word I had used in place of respect. She was obviously disappointed in my response. I could see that. In Crystal's eyes I still didn't quite get it. Politeness wasn't the same thing as respect.

"You'll get it," she said, as though reading my thoughts. "It takes a while. Hey, I've got a great cleaning project for you today . . . if you would like to? Cleaning up this office space."

She gestured around her at all the stuff covering every surface.

"I'd love to!" I blurted out. Another day of cleaning — far from scary registers.

Crystal smiled at my enthusiasm.

"Cool," she said. "I've just got to run out front for a few minutes and check and make sure things are okay. Then I'll be back, and we can get this space really clean!"

Crystal stood up, her fancy black shoes catching my eye.

She hurried toward the front of the store. Crystal always did everything with such positive energy.

I could use some of that forward motion, I thought to myself.

I had a sudden memory of my friend Gordon Fairburn, who had been so full of forward motion during his far too brief life. I pictured the last time I had visited Gordon, and the leave-taking. I was in the driveway of his home, heading toward my

115

car. He was upstairs in his bed, surrounded by his wife and children, dying of prostate cancer. The window of his second-story bedroom looked out over his driveway and was open to the spring day. I heard his high, beautiful voice singing out an old song to me: "Happy trails to you . . . till we meet again!"

I sang the last verse with him. We sang that last song together. Then I got in my car, flung my hand out in the window in a salute of a wave, and drove away. We had been singing many songs since he was at Buckley with me. Gordon was my only friend at that school. We had also been in the same class at Yale. Many nights in New Haven had ended with Gordon at the piano and me and other friends leaning against it, singing old songs. Even after college, we used to love to get together just to laugh and sing. Gordon was my oldest friend. That spring day several years ago he was dying. Now he was dead.

Why was I suddenly thinking of him after Crystal's talk to me?

I had missed him so this last year, when my life was falling apart. Gordon always had a sense of humor, even about the toughest times. He liked to quote a Viennese girl he had been in love with the summer we graduated from college. When she left him, she said, "It is tragic, but not serious."

Gordon had a good perspective on things. I had gone into advertising, and Gordon had gone on to Yale Divinity School and then became a successful therapist, a job he had loved.

Gordon, like Crystal, had a hard early life. His father had been an alcoholic and his parents divorced when he was young. He was physically fragile. Yet he always loved to sing, and loved life. *How Gordon would have loved to still be alive!* I thought. He would have loved to have helped me with my problems, directing me to see them in a better light. He would have loved even to have had the chance to *have* my problems.

I laughed out loud. The sound echoed loudly in the small office space. I looked around quickly. No one had heard me. Crystal and Kester were still up front with the rest of the Partners. It was time for me to grab my green apron, put it on, and get ready to help Crystal with her latest cleaning project.

Maybe it was about time I respected this extra time I had been given. I was not dead, like my beloved friend. I could still sing, and laugh. *Maybe,* I thought, *I had better spend more time singing and laughing, and less time crying about the past.*

My memory of Gordon singing with such courage even in the face of certain death reminded me of how stupid I was being. I should stop taking myself so seriously. Yes, I had lost a lot. I had been through a lot. But I was still in the midst of life at this Starbucks store, and had been treated with respect by Crystal. I had learned there was a lot of dignity in the hardest kind of work. Even cleaning toilets! I should sing and laugh more. Out of respect for Gordon and his amazing, uplifting life. Out of respect for Crystal and what she was teaching me. Out of respect for myself and my new life.

4

On the Front Lines
— Ready or Not

"Let go your sadness, give up the fight,
follow your madness and take flight . . .
take flight."
— lyric by Seal, a musician, published on
the side of a Venti Americano

June

During the next weeks, rushing through
Grand Central Station to catch the shuttle
to the West Side so I could take the subway
up to my Broadway store, I would sometimes be reminded of my previous life when
I had helped in a small way to preserve this
space.

Twenty-five years ago, I had stood in
Grand Central with Jackie Kennedy and my
father as we talked of plans to save the station from destruction. I had been asked to
join them because they wanted me to get
the publicity resources of the J. Walter
Thompson Company behind this effort —

at no cost.

"This is the greatest public space in New York," my father had said, gesturing enthusiastically around him. "It must be preserved."

As my father had aged, he had become more and more passionate about preserving the city he loved. He liked to describe himself as an "architect manqué," always claiming that architecture and buildings were his first love, although that particular phrase and way of describing himself had gotten him into trouble once at an Andy Warhol party. Viva, one of Andy's beautiful, exotic "models" had come up to the group surrounding my father. She was so tall and striking looking that everyone stopped talking. Clearly the center of attention, she took a step toward my father. (Andy himself was as usual sitting on the floor by the wall, saying nothing.)

"What do you do?" the exotic creature asked my father.

"I am an architect manqué!" my father responded in the typical exuberant, confident posture he took in public.

"An architect *monkey?*" she asked.

The room exploded in laughter at her charming mistake.

Yet my father actually *was* a kind of architect monkey — climbing with exuberant physical energy over every beloved structure while jabbering with contagious delight about every stone and the carving of every cornice.

Now he stood poised on the steps overlooking the grand concourse, his arms flung wide in a loving embrace of everything he saw.

"We cannot let this great public space be desecrated by the greedy, opportunistic developers," my father intoned with his melodic baritone, as though speaking to a large audience, although it was just Jackie and me. "It deserves to *be* . . . to *live* as kind of beautiful, open oasis in this crowded, cacophonous city . . . a rare gift of welcoming space for countless *future* generations of New Yorkers."

Jackie stood at his side with adoring eyes. My father was a successful writer, something she had always wanted to be. In addition, he was funny and a social asset, qualities that she could admire. I said little, but already having checked with the powers that be at JWT, I was happy to pledge the company's pro bono support to this effort. Jackie's name was magic to everyone.

I helped organize a train ride by Jackie

with the media down to Washington, where the Supreme Court was due to rule on a historic landmarks preservation law. The event was to be followed by an elegant party to which I invited many notables. Nobody refused my invitations.

Vice President Mondale and his wife, Joan, were happy to greet Jackie as she stepped off the train. We had a reception for her in a small, beautiful room at Washington's Union Station — filled with senators, media, and, most important, a few wives of the justices on the Supreme Court.

(When I met Justice Potter Stewart at a Skull & Bones event a few months later and thanked him for his positive ruling on the landmarks issue, he said, "Don't thank me — it was my wife. She told me I could not vote against Jackie!")

Jackie worked the whole room with an amazing talent for connecting and elevating everyone she spoke to.

As we watched her give her undivided attention to each VIP in the room, my father commented to me, "She has an uncanny gift for managing her own iconography. She is very wise about only committing her great popular appeal to a few causes she really believes in. Fortunately, New York City is a place she really feels passionate about."

Jackie's focused persuasive powers were obvious. She even found time for a few words with me at the end of the event.

"Michael, you have been so helpful."

I had to lean forward to hear her — Jackie talked in a whisper — and I was enveloped in the cocoon of her attention. She made me feel as though I was the only person in the room. She was much more beautiful in person than on television. Smaller, perfect, with wide eyes that seemed to pull you in. There was also a seductive sexiness about her one-on-one that no camera could really capture.

"Thank you," I said, tongue-tied just as even many professional politicians and media mavens were in her powerful presence.

Jackie moved on within seconds, without somehow making me feel any less for the pressure she felt to see and thank others. Quite the reverse. I felt uplifted by those few moments with her, and have never forgotten them.

But I remembered now, glancing at the big, newly sparkling clock above the information booth, and the gleaming, restored space she had achieved in Grand Central, that I could be late for my work. I rushed for the shuttle, knowing that the express subway trains uptown were never there when you needed them.

Fortunately, a train came quickly, and I rode up to Ninety-sixth Street in a grateful jangle of swaying noise and screeching rails.

As I hurried to my store at Ninety-third and Broadway, I was already sweating slightly in the June heat. The summer seemed to have come early to New York, or was it just my own barely subdued sense of panic that was making the heat rise from the pavements of the city?

I made my way into the store, nodding a quick grimace of a smile at my new Partners, and hustled to the back to put on my apron. I clocked in and noticed that at 2 p.m. I had come within minutes of being late. I literally shuddered with the thought. Why had I wasted precious time in Grand Central contemplating the past and almost fucked up my future? I was furious with myself, and I promised that I would give myself more time next time.

Less past, more future! I kept telling myself, a kind of mantra I wanted to believe.

I saw Crystal look up from her computer, and I realized I must have spoken out loud to myself. I was going nuts! Fortunately, she quickly turned back to her computer screen.

Anxious to prove myself, I still hesitated in going out front with the other Partners. Over two months and I had yet to handle a cash register. The thought terrified me. So I just stood there in the neutral zone of Crystal's tiny office space, hoping to be assigned more cleaning today. One more day away from those dreaded cash registers. Yet Crystal seemed barely to notice me. She was so involved with her computer.

Ever glamorous, her lustrous hair fell to her shoulders perfectly, and she wore expensive gold jewelry on each hand. I stood behind her hoping to catch her attention. Crystal had a rare ability to focus despite anyone else being in her little office space. Over her shoulder, I could see that she was preparing some kind of presentation.

I could not resist trying to help.

"In my previous life, I prepared a lot of presentations," I told her. "Maybe I can help."

She turned to me with an annoyed expression. I realized that — for her — I was an unwanted interruption today. Maybe she had just been kind to me on all those previous times — finding something helpful for me to do that also needed doing. But she was clearly out of time, and out of patience, with me.

"Mike, isn't it about time you got out front, and onto a register?"

My mouth literally dropped open. *No!* That wasn't the reaction I had expected to my offer to help her with *her* job.

"You've done the computer simulation, right?" Crystal continued. I had done the training on the computer, but I was sure it was nothing like the actual experience of handling hundreds of dollars while calling drinks and trying to make eye contact with guests.

"Yes . . . ," I reluctantly sounded.

"Good."

"But, Crystal, honest, maybe I could help with your presentation?" I was almost begging to do something I knew how to do, rather than be sent to do something I felt I was certain to fail at.

"How?" She was annoyed again. "This is a presentation about the store and a review of the Partners and how they are doing, and sales of the pastries, and coffee, and beans, and how the physical space is being taken care of . . . not something you know a lot about."

She was being sarcastic, rare for Crystal. She turned back to the screen, clearly trying to dismiss me.

At this point, I wasn't going to let myself

be dismissed. I would do anything to not have to go out to register duty. "Have you heard of KISS?"

"No." She did not look at me and continued focused on the computer. "What does that have to do with what I'm trying to do? Mike, this is tough, I don't have —"

"KISS is a fact based on research about presentations. . . ."

She turned to me. The word "research" had always gotten the attention of clients, and now it worked with Crystal. Any opinion was much more interesting if you preceded it with the idea that there was some scientific study behind it. But I realized I did not want to be pompous with Crystal, as I might have been with my previous clients.

"It's not a big deal," I said. "KISS just stands for 'Keep It Simple, Stupid.' Studies show that the best presentations are simple, and short. Have you ever wished a presentation were *longer,* or more *complicated?*"

Crystal laughed.

Phew. I had also found in my previous life in advertising that if you could get clients to laugh, they usually bought your ideas. Sometimes I had gone to almost any length to get that laugh. Once, in a new business pitch for Sprint, I had taken an extreme approach. We were the last of about eight agencies they were looking at. I knew they would be tired. We were scheduled to go on at three o'clock in the afternoon. The siesta time, biologically the worst time to present anything, let alone ask a company to trust you — a new agency — with millions of dollars in advertising. In the request for proposal Sprint had asked the question "What would you do if someone made a mistake on our account?"

That gave me an idea.

To start our presentation I said, "We have answered every one of the thirty-three questions in your RFP. In detail. We will hand you out copies to study over the next few days. We know we are the last agency of many. And you have probably heard many promises. So we will simply address some key questions. We will not *promise* you anything. We will *demonstrate* in the next few minutes exactly how we would handle your account. We will present actual ad ideas, already tested in focus groups and ready to go. We will present a real media plan that can save you money." I paused for effect. "But, first, we want to address one of the most important questions in your RFP: What would we do if someone made a mistake on your account? Here's our an-

128

swer. Last night an account executive, Harry Smink, who is now in this room, misspelled your name on one of our submissions. Here's what's coming to you, Harry."

At that point I pulled out a real pistol with a blank in it and shot him. He pretended to fall over. The clients were shocked, woke up, and laughed out loud. They were very attentive, maybe even a little scared not to pay attention throughout our presentation. We won the account.

Laughter was good. So I was glad that Crystal laughed now.

"So how do I do KISS?" she said, always quick to recognize an opportunity that might help her.

I knew I did not have much time.

"You could try the three P's."

She gave me a look as much to say: *Get on with it!*

"People. Product. Profits. You could talk about the new people you've hired; under Product could be the pastries and bean sales; and Profits is the bottom line for all those three things coming together."

"Plus *Place*," Crystal said, reaching up to slap my hand with a high five. I slapped back, hard and clumsy in my enthusiasm. We did not high-five at JWT.

She turned to her screen.

129

"Place?" I asked.

"The store . . . we've done some cleaning here, Mike, as you well know . . . I want to highlight that as well."

Stupidly, I could not resist arguing with her. My expertise had told me otherwise. "But research shows that people can only remember three things. No one, after hundreds of years, can remember more than three of the Ten Commandments."

"Say what?" Crystal hadn't really been listening. I was thankful, and decided to shut up. After *one* more suggestion. I couldn't help myself.

"The best presentations start with some surprising visual or prop . . . something that they will never forget."

I was thinking of a presentation I had done about a name change on an airline. No one in the Allegheny Airlines management wanted to change the name. It was expensive to change, and people, contrary to myth, hate any kind of change. But I hated the name Allegheny. And so did most customers. They called it Agony Airlines. When I had met the chairman, who was a fragile man in his late seventies, his first question to me was "What do you think of the name of my airline?"

"If it was neutral you could stay with it,

but it's not good to be a joke."

He didn't buy it at first. Then we did the usual mind-changing name research that showed that people would wait thirty minutes to take USAir, a then as yet nonexistent airline, rather than Allegheny.

One morning I was asked to present the name change idea to the chairman and five hundred sales reps from across the country. It was a huge, drafty room, part of an aircraft hangar. Not a great place to make a pitch.

I started with the research. Dead silence. I could sense the room wasn't buying it.

But I had bought props the previous night. A baseball bat and a baseball. I had never liked baseball, and played it terribly in high school. It wasn't a rational decision, but I knew I had to do something to shake this audience up. They were set in their ways, lovers of the status quo.

I took up the bat.

I said, "This name change is going to let us knock the competition out of the park."

I threw the ball up and tried to hit a long, high fly ball. Instead, in my nervousness, I hit a powerful straight shot, almost grazing the head of the chairman. He was in the front row of seats stretching back almost a hundred yards, filled with his sales force.

He threw himself to the floor. The ball raced to the back of the room and gave off a great *whack* when it hit the metal wall in the back.

There was dead silence for a moment, then the whole sales team almost as one person rose and roared with a deafening cheer. It occurred to me that perhaps they were just excited by seeing their chairman nearly get beaned (he was not beloved). Maybe they were tired of losing to the competition year after year, and I had sparked some bloodlust. Whatever happened, that ball slamming into the far wall gave us a room full of new emotion.

They were ready to move forward.

We sold the new name.

But we couldn't have done it without the bat and the ball.

"Before you get to your PowerPoint four P's presentation," I said to Crystal, enunciating the "four" for her benefit, "isn't there some prop you could hold up . . . just so they get a sense of who you are? Something to make it memorable. Remember, your audience will be seeing lots of presentations about lots of stores."

She looked at me.

Then I saw her beautiful eyes sparkle with an idea.

"How about this: I still have the first

pound of coffee I ever ground, from seven years ago. I keep it in my apartment as a thing."

"A thing what?" I asked.

"Just a thing. It means a lot to me."

"Why?"

"I don't know. Maybe because it was part of joining Starbucks and turning my life around. I kept it. That pound of ground Verona coffee means a lot to me."

"Great."

I knew that Crystal's love for that first pound of coffee would resonate with her audience. But who *was* her audience?

"Whom are you presenting to?"

"A lot of district managers, and other store managers."

"Perfect. Just start your presentation by holding up the pound of coffee. Wait till they are quiet. Then say how it turned your life around."

"Cool," Crystal said, turning back to her computer. "Now get out to the registers, Mike. Joann is out there. . . . She is patient. Let her help you get going."

Shit! After all my effort to avoid the register by helping Crystal with her presentation, something I was good at, I was still going to be forced to do the money part of the business, at which I knew I would fail.

133

Literally dragging my feet, I made my way out to the front of the store. Fortunately, it was the one quiet part of the afternoon, just after lunch and before the schoolkids piled in for their Frappuccinos.

There were three registers behind the counter. Bianca was on the one closest to the pastry case, there was an empty one in the middle, and Joann was on the register by the bar. I walked by Bianca, toward the middle register.

"Hi, Mike," she said.

There were no Guests.

I stopped, eager for any chance to avoid that register.

"Hi, Bianca. How are you?"

"Good." Bianca had a sweet face and was very small. Her voice was so soft I could hardly hear her.

I made my way to "my" register.

"Joann," I said, "Crystal told me you'd help me get a register."

"Sure, Mike."

Joann was a large, comforting woman and older than most Partners. She moved slowly, compared to the others. I could hear her breathe as she came up to me. She didn't sound well.

"You okay?"

"Yes," she said, "I just breathe hard."

"Just punch in your numbers on the screen," she said, "then take the register drawer to the back. There's a machine that will weigh the cash — should be one hundred fifty dollars in your drawer. Then come on back."

A machine that will weigh and count the cash! My heart leapt with joy. I had never heard of such a thing. I was almost ready to cry with gratitude. Counting out pennies and dollars would have taken me hours, and I would have gotten the sum wrong. I always did.

I grabbed the drawer and headed toward the back. Crystal was still very involved in her presentation, but she looked up with a smile when she saw me.

"There's the weighing machine," Crystal said, pointing toward a small desktop instrument. "Just put your coins and paper on that, and make sure it comes out to exactly one hundred fifty. You'll be responsible for any over or under. By the way, you are not allowed to be, at the end of the shift, more than five dollars over or under."

"Sounds good," I said, not realizing that when you process a thousand dollars, you can easily be several dollars short or long.

I started to put my paper on the weighing machine. It was about the size of a large hardcover book. It had a metal pocket on top in which you put your bills. Your coins were already in little pockets in your register, and you just lifted them out and the magical machine weighed them up exactly as well. For example, if you put a bunch of dollar bills on, a little window would read underneath: $85. Or if you put a pocket of pennies on from your register, the machine would read: $0.50. The simple machine kept a running count, and at the end it showed on a little screen beneath the pocket the exact amount weighed. I was not required to add or subtract anything! And by weighing the currency and the coins, the machine made what could have been a time-consuming and laborious task into a matter of just a minute or two. To me, on that first day at the register, the little weighing machine was a major miracle. The count was exact, and I turned to head back toward the register, a little more confident.

"Hey, Mike," Crystal called after me.

I stopped and turned my head.

"The presentation looks good. What do I do for an ending?" I felt pleased she was asking me for advice, for anything. That was a first with Crystal and me.

I walked back, still holding the drawer of

the register. I stopped to put it down on the desk.

"Don't ever let the money out of your hands. That's a good rule," Crystal said in her best professional voice.

I picked the drawer back up.

"The best ending is a summary of what you've said, Crystal. A quick summary. I'd just put up the three P's —"

"The four P's, remember? . . . We added Place to People, Product, and Profits."

"Okay." I smiled inside. She had gotten it, and she had said "we," which was a nice nod to me. "So put up a slide of the four P's, and then an equal sign . . . and then the words 'Starbucks Success.' "

"That sounds too cold," Crystal said. Now she had become the expert. I was used to this. Almost all ad clients took about ten minutes to decide they knew better than you. But I had to admit to myself she might have a point. Starbucks was not IBM. We were selling coffee with love, a positive, emotional experience, not machines with an objective expertise.

"So what *do* all those things equal?" I asked, maybe a little bit defensively. I still was clinging to my last vestiges of the fancy corporate guy who knew what he was doing. At least in this one area, I still felt a need to show off.

Crystal thought for a moment and then suggested, "How about we put up the four P's, and then the equal sign, and then the words 'Great Experience for Our Guests.' "

"Okay," I said, turning to go.

"But you don't like it," Crystal called.

"Well, to me the unique thing about Starbucks is what a great experience it is for the *Partners*. Every Fortune 500 company says they put the customer first. Starbucks puts the Partners first."

Crystal looked at me. Her eyebrows drew together as she thought. Then her face relaxed.

"Okay, how about this: The equal sign leads to 'Great Experience for Partners and Guests.' "

"Good," I said, heading out to the registers. I felt a need to get out while the getting was good. Crystal understood the idea; she'd put together a professional presentation. I remembered my mantra: *Less past, more future.* Anything more I said would be just because I liked to live in my past life, rather than make a future. The register was waiting, and I felt that kindly Joann would help me make it through.

But I literally stopped mid-step, holding my drawer.

"How about," I couldn't resist saying, " 'The Best Experience for Partners and Guests.' It's more euphonious."

"What is . . . euphony . . . ?" Crystal was frowning.

"Forget it." I kept walking.

"No," Crystal called. "Remember: dignity and respect? You got something to say, say it." Her tone was not positive.

I felt I had put my foot in it. *Such a pompous fool,* I told myself. I turned back to her.

" 'Euphonious' just means sounds good," I told her in an apologetic tone. " 'Best' is a word that kind of rhymes with Guest . . . makes the last summation sound more memorable. Research shows people remember rhymes easier. That means after seeing a bunch of presentations, they will be more likely to remember yours."

"Okay," Crystal said, " 'The *Best* Experience for Partners and *Guests.*' "

"And when you use the word 'the' in front of something like that, it implies a preemptive benefit."

Crystal wasn't listening anymore — thank goodness.

"Get out to the registers, Mike," she encouraged me. "And be sure to make eye contact, and connect with conversation."

I had heard those words on the training

video, but I was more concerned with just handling the cash so that I did not make a perfect fool of myself.

Unfortunately, now the kids from school had arrived.

Joann came over to me, though, and helped me put my drawer in.

"The computer will show you the correct change, and the great thing is the Guest will see the numbers too, so they can catch you if you get it wrong. You'll do fine, Mike."

"But I'm terrible with money."

"So were my first two husbands. But just let the register do the work."

I smiled. A good mantra.

A kid stepped up to my register to order. He had no idea he was dealing with a guy who had never done this before.

"I want a Tall Mocha."

I called down to Tawana, an attractive but combative barista on the espresso bar: "Tall Mocha."

"Tall Mocha," Tawana called back to me, confirming she had gotten the order right.

I looked at the register. On the screen read the words "Tall" and "Mocha," just like on the computer-training module. I jabbed at them with my finger. Sure enough, it worked, and the price came up on my screen.

The boy handed me five dollars.

The screen displayed the option "Five dollars" in a box.

I punched at the box.

The register then opened, and the screen displayed the exact change I should hand him: "$2.73." I dug out the change from my drawer. The kid looked at it and stuck it in his pocket, and made his way to the espresso bar to pick up his drink.

My screen, about the size of a small television, read: "Close your drawer."

I closed my drawer.

Hey, I said to myself, *you can do this!*

Then the next Guest stepped up, a young lady who was clearly pregnant.

"Just a Decaf Tall Coffee," she said.

I punched in Tall, took her money, gave her the change, closed the drawer, and turned to get a cup of coffee for her. Fresh coffee was right behind me, with the cups. I gave one to her.

She gave me a big smile, as though I were already a friend. "My name's Rachel. I have another child on the way. I have to stick to Decaf for a while. Can't wait to get back on the hard stuff."

I had a sudden realization that people might treat me the way they were said to treat bartenders. . . . They wanted to engage with someone serving them the good stuff.

The afternoon went surprisingly well, despite the constant stream of customers.

As evening fell, it got even busier, but Joann came over a couple of times to help me out. The line moved smoothly, with people ordering Single Pump Mocha or Tall Latte. I was supposed to call out the *size,* name of drink, and any "customizing" such as: One Tall One Pump Mocha. Often I would get the order wrong, and start with One Pump Mocha, forgetting to call the size . . . or call for a Tall Latte forgetting to mention the Guest wanted it with skim milk. Sometimes Guests would order Single Pump Mocha or they would order a drink backward, starting with the milk, then the syrup, then the size, and I would repeat what they said and call it out to Tawana. Tawana would correct me at the top of her lungs, putting the order in the right way. It was humiliating for me, but I learned fast.

Also, it was a gift to me that Tawana had such a large, commanding voice. With my brain tumor that affected my hearing, I had been worried about getting the orders straight, and I never missed Tawana's powerful calls. And I found that by leaning over the register, closer to the Guests, I could also hear them clearly.

"Ask if you have any questions," Joann said. "Just ask."

And I did. I found that the Guests didn't seem to mind helping me get their request just right.

That night, around 7 p.m., I was surprised to see the store grow really busy. I had thought coffee was something you picked up on the way to work, but it clearly was now an essential pick-me-up on the way home as well. I noticed a businessman enter the store and join the growing line. When I had been on the *other* side of the bar, I had worked so hard just to get a prospective client like this well-dressed man to return a call. Now my customers were literally waiting in line for my services, I thought to myself. How funny.

The businessman stepped up in line and told me, "Double Macchiato."

Starbucks language. I had a hard time figuring out what it translated to on the cash register screen. I started to feel flushed as I punched at various combinations incorrectly.

"You are new here, right?" the man asked. I looked at him. Was he going to complain to Crystal and get me fired on my first day at the register?

But he smiled at my look of panic.

"Don't worry, you'll get it."

He actually took the time to encourage me. Wow. I looked back at the screen with a renewed clarity of mind. Double Macchiato. Hit Tall, then Macchiato. Simple.

The businessman wasn't the only one to try to set me at ease.

"Welcome to the neighborhood," one lady said.

Another guy with an open shirt who looked like a hippie commented, "I'm glad to see they are hiring older people."

Older?! Okay, so I wasn't so happy with this comment, but I appreciated his attitude. No denying it: I was older, at least a generation or two older than most Partners, so it was good to be welcomed even if it was for my conspicuous seniority.

Around eight o'clock it started to get even busier. I had not realized that people had made Starbucks a part of their nightlife. Crowds of young people were piling in to share time with one another over their Lattes.

Focus, I reminded myself. *Punch the right button, call out the order, make the right change, smile.* A beautiful young blond woman came up to my register.

"A Tall Skim Latte," she said.

I intently punched in Tall Latte on my

register, called out the drink to Tawana in the right order, took the young woman's five-dollar bill, and started to hand her back her change. I had looked up to smile when I realized it was my daughter, Annie! I had been concentrating so hard on not making a mistake that I had not even realized who I was serving.

"Hi, Dad," she said, smiling. She obviously thought it was funny that I had not recognized her. Maybe she also thought it was funny to see me in a green apron wearing a black cap, and in a situation in which I was so clearly over my head.

"Annie!" I said. "Good to see you!"

I felt the blood going to my face. Here I was, serving my daughter in a blue-collar job. I could only think in clichés. . . . I could not really *think* at all. But I remembered what Crystal had said about respect, and tried to stand tall and respect myself, and show respect for my daughter. Annie must have realized I was struggling to greet her properly, and that there was a big line of impatient Guests behind her . . . eager to order their drinks.

She confidently took charge of the situation. "I'll wait. . . . What time are you off?"

"Nine . . . I'll be off at nine."

"See you then," she said, heading off to

pick up her drink at the espresso bar. Annie was clearly more at ease in a Starbucks store than I was.

"Double Tall Skim No Whip Mocha," the next young lady said. I laboriously hit the different keys on the screen, and called the drink out to Tawana. She called it back exactly the same way, and I was relieved. The Guest had known what she was doing.

You know how it is when you are involved in some sport or physical activity when you can't stop and you can't think about anything else? I remembered when I had played football in high school. Just like now, I really didn't know what I was doing, but the effort, the mud, the tackling and pushing and shoving carried me along. If you had been a spectator, you would have seen me as willing but not very good. Probably I was performing the same way now. The rest of the night passed in a blur.

As the night wound down, Joann went home to her child. Crystal appeared behind me. "It's time, Mike," she called. "Pull your till."

"Pull the grill?"

Crystal cracked up and turned to Bianca. "He said pull his grill!"

Though I protested, I actually liked that they laughed at me. At least they felt comfortable in my presence.

Crystal showed me how to weigh my money out.

"Your 'drop' should be the total weighed out, minus one hundred fifty. Don't worry, the machine will tell you the amount."

And the machine did. It also said, on the computer, that I was $4.50 short.

"Not too bad for your first time," Crystal said. "As I said, you are allowed to be five dollars over or under . . . but most Partners come within a few cents. You'll get it."

Was she out of her mind? She had no idea of the financial idiot she was talking to. But I was grateful I had just gotten through the terrible experience. There was almost nothing I had enjoyed about the register itself, although I was surprised what a high I had gotten from interacting with the Guests who were so eager to buy from me.

"You did okay, Mike," Crystal said in review as she oversaw my weighing out. "But try to call out the drinks correctly. And I was watching you. You usually made eye contact, but you hardly made any conversation with the Guests. I understand you can't do much when there is a line, but if you get the time, try to say a few words. A lot of people come to Starbucks to feel better. . . .

It's part of our job to make them feel better."

"Sure," I said, just grateful not to have been hundreds of dollars short.

Crystal looked at her wrist.

"I gotta go," she said, pulling on a fancy leather coat. "Punch out, Mike," she called back to me as she headed to the front.

I had noticed a black Corvette idling out front, and it occurred to me that it was waiting for her. Crystal sure was glamorous. I watched as she stopped on the way out the door to talk with several Guests. Even though someone was waiting for her, she obviously put her job first.

I punched out on the time clock on her computer . . . 9:05. I had put in seven hours. My feet ached, and my head was still spinning.

Then I remembered: Annie! She was waiting for me. I pulled off my apron quickly and made my way out front.

I found her around a corner, at a small table, reading a book.

"Hi, Annie."

"Daddy!" She leapt up from the table and gave me a big hug.

I felt much better.

"Would you like another Latte?" I said.

"No," she laughed, "let's go. . . . It's late

148

for you."

Annie knew that I usually liked to get to bed early. I am more of a lark than an owl, and when she was growing up, Annie and I would share the early hours together. When she was two or three, we would walk down to the little lake in Connecticut in the fresh dawn of the summer mornings. I would splash with her in the shallows and watch the sun come up behind the pine trees. Then we would walk home and share some cereal before the rest of the family woke up.

We walked toward the door of my store, and Annie took my arm. That made me feel better.

Out of the corner of my eye, I noticed that Crystal was still busy chatting with some Guests. Impressive.

"We'll take the subway down to Times Square," Annie said, taking charge of me, "the shuttle over to Grand Central, and I can get a subway back to Brooklyn from there. And you can get a train to Bronxville."

Annie had it all figured out. She was a hard worker who had become a great student and graduated Phi Beta Kappa from college, but had decided to be an actress, and she brought to that profession all her positive organizational abilities.

As we rode the rocking subway downtown, we talked over the jangling noise.

"I wanted to see if you were *really* working at Starbucks," Annie explained. I had told her mother and left a message for Annie that I was working at the Broadway store but telling her to *wait* for a while, until I was better at my job. She hadn't waited.

Annie was born without a willing-to-wait gene in her body. I remember when she was three, she had said to me: "I want to ride a horse."

"Fine," I said. "Someday you can."

"Now."

"You're too small."

Annie was an athletic little girl . . . but still way too small in my eyes to handle a dangerous beast like a horse.

"Please," she said, and repeated it so often that I finally decided to prove to her that riding a horse was out of the question for a little girl her age.

I took her to a riding school and had the owner talk to her. We sat down in his office. He was behind a big desk and looked very imposing to me. Annie was not awed.

"I want to ride," she said, getting off of my lap and standing before him. Annie always stood very straight.

"I'm sorry, young lady," he said. "We

don't take anyone under five."

Annie looked at him for a moment and then repeated her request, more loudly. Along with Annie's persistence she also had quite a temper. She was born with a face that reminded me of the late photos of Queen Victoria: rather pudgy but with her mouth turned down in an "I am not amused" expression. It was a year after she was born before Annie really smiled, despite all our best efforts. She had a beautiful smile, but her usual expression was one of serious determination.

The man leaned forward on his desk.

"I admire your attitude," he said, "but I'm afraid you are too young."

"Please!" Annie said. I could sense we were going to have a temper tantrum, and maybe he could too. Annie was unequaled in her ability to throw herself into a temper tantrum. She would seem out of control, but actually she could stop on a dime once she got her way. Annie had more or less been in control since she arrived in my life. Maybe this man who owned the riding school was beginning to realize what a powerful person this three-year-old was.

"I tell you what I'm going to do," he said, coming around the desk and taking Annie's hand. She was a cute little girl with lots of blond hair — hard to resist.

Together, they went out to the horse ring.

He called over a young woman who was leading a horse around.

"Amanda," he said, "bring Trigger over. I want to show this young lady something."

Maybe he hoped the huge beast that approached us would scare Annie. *I* was scared. I had never liked horses and Trigger looked way too big for *anyone* to ride.

"Would you like to try to ride that horse, young lady?" the owner asked with a kind of condescending tone.

Annie didn't say anything. She just ran right over and tried to get on.

Amanda helped her into the saddle, laughing. It was clear that Amanda was on Annie's side.

"Take it easy, Amanda," the big man said. "She is only three."

"Looks like she's ready," Amanda said, beginning to lead the horse very slowly around the ring. Amanda put the reins in Annie's hands, although she still held on to the bridle.

"Shit," the man said under his breath, although I could hear him.

I looked at him.

"She's got a lot of spirit," he said. "Okay, we'll do it. Amanda can handle it."

He turned and went back to his office, leaving me standing there watching Annie and Amanda move slowly around the ring.

Annie had won. She had not waited patiently to be allowed to ride. So I was not surprised that she had shown up to see me despite my plea for *no one* to come until I had mastered my job.

"I just wanted to see if it was really true," Annie laughed.

"Well," I said, defensively, "it's a job."

"No, don't get me wrong," Annie said. "I like it. You look good in that black cap."

I sensed that while she was teasing a little bit, she wasn't kidding. Maybe she liked the idea I was willing to work hard. And it must have been clear to her that I was struggling, which she obviously didn't mind.

"I still don't know what I'm doing," I said.

"I know. . . . You looked like that!" she laughed. I laughed. I was filled with love for this wonderful person, and with regret.

"Annie," I said with deep sincerity, "I am so sorry that I've messed up my life so, and *your* life. . . ."

It was as if I had reminded her of a fact she had forgotten, and suddenly, the goodwill seemed to dissipate. She said angrily, "I'll never listen to your stupid advice again."

The subway pulled into Times Square, and as we exited, Annie pointed us toward the shuttle, where we were transferring.

As we sat in the shuttle waiting for it to take us to Grand Central, I broke the silence. "I'm sorry," I said again.

"Sorry doesn't cut it," Annie said. She had always had a great temper.

The shuttle filled up with people. I let an old lady with five shopping bags take my seat. Annie also stood up. We were squeezed together with hundreds of others.

Annie was wearing an elegantly styled coat, and her posture was straight despite the crush of people and the swaying car, and she seemed so bright and beautiful — even under the harsh fluorescent lights. She was so put together. I looked down at my shoes, hating the idea that I had lost the respect of my intelligent, hardworking daughter by my stupid, selfish acts.

We got out in Grand Central. As we passed by the warm lights of the Oyster Bar, I was tempted to invite Annie to have something to eat with me. But then I remembered sitting in my accountant's office at tax time just a few weeks before.

Lawrence Best had helped me and many successful advertising people with their money, but I had told him in the last year

154

that I could not pay him for his services. He said he wanted to help me anyway. When I brought in my tax records, I brought two Starbucks gift cards for his kids. Larry was gracious in his acceptance of this tiny remuneration.

"My kids will love these," he said. "They don't know what I do, really. But I know they love Starbucks. And they are away at college, so they will like using these."

"Now," he said, "looking at your American Express records, I see you are charging meals at the Oyster Bar."

"Yes, well, it's on my way home from Starbucks."

"But," Larry said, leaning forward, "the thing is, you are not a big advertising hotshot on an expense account anymore. You are working at Starbucks for what? Ten bucks an hour? The thing is, you can't afford to eat *one* oyster for that amount!"

Larry sat back and pointed to a small paper bag on his crowded desk.

"That's my lunch."

I got his point.

So I pushed away thoughts of treating Annie to a late meal at the Oyster Bar. Yet I did want to apologize to her. I remembered Crystal's emphasis on dignity and respect and realized that I had not treated Annie or any one of my children with the respect and dignity that they deserved. I had been a pompous fool broadcasting advice while my own life was falling apart.

I stopped walking with Annie, looked into her clear blue eyes, and said: "I am sorry for being such a pompous fool."

She reached over and gave me a hug.

"You *have* been stupid, but I like your working at Starbucks."

I felt a great sense of relief. Annie had a quick temper, but an equally fast ability to forgive and move on. I had once told her: "You are like a summer thunderstorm."

"What do you mean?" Annie had asked.

"Your temper is so strong and quick."

"But it's great after that kind of summer storm . . . a fresh new feeling to everything!" Annie had replied, winning the dialogue as usual.

Now she looked up at the big schedule board listing all the trains.

"I am going down this corridor to catch a subway to Brooklyn," she said. "Your next train for Bronxville leaves in four minutes. Don't miss it."

Then she gave me a strong hug and a kiss, and I ran for my train with a lighter heart.

5
Open Wide and Smile — You're on Broadway

"I have resigned myself to having less and less resolute opinions."
— a quote from Amel Larrieux, singer-songwriter, published on the side of a Tall Chai Latte

July–August

I awoke, sweating. I had no air conditioner and my little attic apartment was sweltering in the summer heat. It was only 3:00 a.m. I had an hour or so before I had to get up and leave for New York, but I was too hot and anxious about helping Crystal open the store for the first time to go back to sleep.

I could feel my heart beating, which scared me. The idea of opening with Crystal was really getting to me. I told myself to calm down, but some conversations I had overheard made me worry. Other Partners had said, "Opening is a bitch," and similar comments that made me feel it might be more than I could handle.

I tried to remind myself that in my previous life I loved challenges. I loved going after new business or meeting a "tough" client. But opening a store was a physical challenge. I had never been confident physically.

Suddenly, I had a bad memory come into my head of a physical challenge I should have avoided. But the stupid physical test came at a time when I was still an adolescent and had too much to prove to resist the challenge.

Sweating in the summer heat, I remembered a scary time in Spain, in 1959. When I was just nineteen, taking the summer to go to Europe by myself. I could now almost still feel the hard-packed earth of the campground on the outskirts of Pamplona baking in the unforgiving sun.

Like many young men of the time, I had gone to Spain seeking Papa, and I found him. That summer Ernest Hemingway sat in the center of the sunny square at Pamplona surrounded by an adoring circle of fans from all over the world. He had a handsome face and broad shoulders, with white hair carefully combed over a scar I should never have mentioned.

I stepped up.

"Michael Gill," I said, shaking the hand he extended. His grip was very strong, almost crushing. His eyes were measuring me. He did not ask me to sit down and join the group.

"Janet Flanner sends her regards," I said to him. Janet Flanner was a colleague of my father's on *The New Yorker,* the Paris correspondent, and an old drinking friend of Hemingway's. I had met her a few weeks before. When she found out I was a big fan of Hemingway, she told me to use her name. She also mentioned that I should ask Hemingway about a scar that ran along the top of his head. Rumor had it that he had been hit by a piece of shrapnel in the War, or had gotten gored by a charging rhino in Africa. All Janet Flanner had told me was "There's a good story behind that scar . . . *if* Ernest will tell it."

At the mention of Janet, Ernest Hemingway looked at me with new interest.

"She is a friend of my father's," I explained. "Brendan Gill."

"Yes, I know him," Hemingway said slowly, seeming to measure every word.

"And Janet is an old friend of mine," he said, now with new confidence and loudness, addressing his whole group of eager acolytes in a surprisingly high, tenor voice.

"Or, rather, Janet is a *very* good friend of mine. One of the great reporters of her generation."

I noticed that he did not say "writers." So he was not in competition with Janet Flanner. She was a "reporter," not a "writer." That would explain how they could still be friends. Under his formal courtesy was a hint of aggression.

"Miguel is the son of another friend of mine," Hemingway announced to the larger group, deciding quickly on his nickname for me. "Brendan Gill, a colleague of Janet Flanner's on *The New Yorker* magazine."

A few heads nodded in appreciation. They had heard of my father.

Looking back now, forty-five years later, as I tossed and turned in my hot bed before my morning Starbucks shift, it occurred to me that I had gone to Hemingway for validation. I had used the only means I knew how: my father and his connections. And while these connections had opened the door for me, they hadn't gotten me in. At that moment in Pamplona, it was up to me and me alone to prove myself. And it made me angry.

I had looked Hemingway in the eye, remembering Janet Flanner's comment. "How did you get that scar?" I asked in retaliation, sensing that this question, the whole subject of the scar, was one that would annoy him. Hemingway's eyes went dead after my question — for just a second. This was a man who was used to being in combat. Actual. And verbal.

Then, ignoring my question, he asked simply, "Have you run before the bulls?"

"No," I said, and then stupidly added, "not yet." I had not thought a moment before that I would risk my life in such a stupid spectacle.

"Well," Hemingway said slowly, calculating his verbal punch, "you run in front of the bulls, Miguel, then come back and we can talk."

He had treated me like a boy, not yet a man.

I stayed up drinking all that night, held aloft by the manic festival atmosphere. By morning, I had decided I *had* to run before the bulls. The bull corral was opened at 7 a.m. each morning, and those foolish enough to do it raced up a mile of cobbled streets to the arena, bulls hot in pursuit the whole way. I dreaded the whole thing.

It was growing light when I got to the corral holding the bulls for the day's corrida. I could hear the bulls moving around, occasionally banging against the boards that contained them. I climbed up the side of the corral to look at them. They all looked big and dark and mean to me.

Soon, a crowd gathered, mostly young men, getting ready for the run.

An old man stood at my side. I nodded to him. Like most Spaniards in Pamplona, he knew I was a stranger here. Although I had very little Spanish, and he had *no* English, I gradually understood that he was urging me to wait farther up the street.

The gang of youths had become louder near the corral. They were clearly primed for this ordeal, and probably quite drunk as well.

The old man indicated again — very energetically — that I should wait for the bulls farther up the hill.

I looked up the hill.

The street was a narrow one, lined by large wooden barricades. I decided to take his advice. The old man had offered me a way out. After all, Hemingway had challenged me to run before the bulls, but he did not indicate *where* I should start the run.

I walked several hundred yards up the hill and leaned against the barricade to rest a moment. Then I sat down. I suddenly realized how tired I was. I had not slept well in days. The first sun was just hitting me. I dozed off.

A commotion behind my barricade woke me. The crowd was gathering there, waiting for the imminent release of the bulls. I clearly didn't have much time. I had an urge to leap over the barricade to safety, and join the onlookers. Hemingway would never know. I resented him now, for forcing me to risk my life in such a stupid adventure.

A loud and big gang was already running toward me. I had nowhere to go. So I was going to be part of the first runners, after all.

Then, suddenly, there was a shout, and everyone began to run, much, much faster than I had expected.

I tried to stay up with the leaders, but gradually dropped toward the middle.

As I came around one corner, I stumbled on the uneven cobblestones and slammed into a barricade. Some hands helped me up. My back felt like it was broken, and my hands were scraped when I tried to right myself.

Hands patted my back and pushed me back into the pack. I found myself running for my life. Somehow, I had gotten a second wind, full of pure, unadulterated fear.

I feared I was going to die on that narrow

street, surrounded by people I did not know, gored by a bull that had no interest in me but simply would aim his horn for my shirt. All in the name of Papa.

I fought my way to the front, lifting my legs high, passing beyond the pain until I was just going on adrenaline. I found myself within two or three men of the very front of the pack. Up ahead I could see the bullfight arena, which gave me extra energy. I did not care about anything but getting there.

I gave a final burst of speed and just as the gates were opened I made it, within seconds of the first people through.

A whole cluster of bulls now charged into the arena. A man fell before them, and some bulls stepped over him, and some stepped on him. Another brave fellow had a cape and was trying to make some passes. The crowd roared approval.

After the last of the bulls had entered, I snuck over to the side of a barricade and went out the same opening the bulls had just come in.

The corridor smelled of bull piss and human sweat.

I could hear screams but also cheers behind me. I was not in the mood to play. I was covered in sweat, still shaking a little from fear. I had not run before the bulls in the traditional way — all the way — but I had done enough. Hemingway had not said how far to run . . . just to run! I rationalized. I had certainly run! I found a small alley that was still dark, unlit by the early morning sun, and I lay down, and whimpered (my back still hurt from slamming into the barricade), and slept.

The sun woke me, creeping down the wall. I went back up to the main square. Hemingway was not at the café at this early hour, so I sat near his big, circular table and ordered a beer.

And another.

I just stared into space. My experience would not be over, I knew, until I told Hemingway about it. Soon after one p.m. Hemingway emerged from the hotel. Each time I saw him, I was impressed again by how large and wide-chested a man he seemed. His swarm of pilot fish followed him, as always, in Pamplona. There was something of the whale or shark about Hemingway. He seemed to move without flapping of arms or legs — just moved forward followed by his eager, fluttering fans.

He sat down, raised his big hand to order, and then he caught sight of me.

"Miguel?" It was not a command, it was a question. Maybe he did not recognize me.

I rose and made myself walk erect over to his table (I ached in every joint).

"I ran in front of the bulls," I said, standing in front of him like some little kid telling his father of a great achievement.

"Good," Papa said, nodding his head. "Good."

He indicated the chair next to him, which had not yet been filled. A great honor.

I took it eagerly, almost collapsing into it.

Hemingway signaled the waiter to bring me a drink.

The crowd sitting around us was, I felt sure, listening hard to hear what he would say to me, but he simply clinked my glass, toasting me as I drank.

Then he leaned forward toward me and said in a low voice, "Now I will tell you about that scar."

Hemingway scraped his chair around and faced me so that no one else gathered at the table could hear what he told me.

"Some people will tell you I got that scar fighting in the War, or in Africa."

Papa spoke deliberately, as though measuring every word. It also occurred to me that, although he had just reached the square, and just had his first drinks there, he might have been drinking earlier, up in his room at the hotel. For he had that sense

166

of profound emphasis that a drunk acquires — as though the whole world rested on the precision of every word. Yet, as serious as his manner was, his eyes still held a combative sparkle.

"Many people make up many stories about Papa," Hemingway said, as though referring to a third person, with a slight, shy smile, "but few know the truth. Here is the truth of the scar, Miguel:

"It was in Paris. A group of us had been drinking all day. Later, we ended up back in someone's place. I went to the bathroom, and reached up to pull the chain to flush the old-fashioned toilet. I was strong in those days, and I reached too far, and pulled too hard. . . . I grabbed the lever to a skylight and pulled the whole damn thing down on my head. The glass smashed on my head. There was a lot of blood. Someone panicked, and insisted I go to a hospital. A French hospital in the middle of the night. They sewed me up, and did a terrible job of it. So I got this scar.

"I never told people of that story, so they made up their own. Like the War. Like an African safari and a lion ripping at my head as I moved in to finish him. But you have heard the true story, Miguel. Now let's have some drinks with our friends."

He turned back to the larger crowd, signaling with his beefy forearm for another round.

Now, in my little attic room, thinking of Hemingway's story of the toilet and the scar, I got out of bed and hobbled on my sore feet to the bathroom and took a shower. I once ran fast from the bulls, but now could hardly handle a job serving coffee, I thought to myself grimly.

My feet hurt all the time since I had joined Starbucks. At first I thought I had the wrong kind of shoes. Fancy black brogues. Then I got a pair of black sneakers (you are allowed to wear any kind of shoe, as long as it's black). But my feet still hurt. Then one of my Partners, a big man named Anthony, told me that I'd be better off with paratrooper boots:

"They use 'em to jump out of planes and land on the ground."

Big boots were in with the Partners.

I spent a lot of my hard-earned money on the combat boots, but my feet hurt even more. My sister Holly, who was the closest in age to me, just two years younger, called, asking, "How's the job at Starbucks?"

"Great, but my feet hurt. I'm on my feet all day."

"You're just getting old," she replied

frankly. "The pads on the bottom of your feet get thinner as you age, and your feet hurt more."

I hung up, feeling even worse. So I went back to my sneakers.

The funny thing was my feet didn't hurt when I was actually working. It was like when I was playing high school football: You didn't notice the aches and pains until after the game. Many summers before, I had come back to Bronxville to train with our high school football team despite the fact that I was a terrible athlete. We had worked out each day in the punishing August heat. I didn't become anything better than a third-string guard on the football team through all that extra effort, but at least I had hardly felt any pain during that difficult physical challenge so long ago. Now I was in a constant state of negotiation with my aching feet.

I had a sudden memory of my son Charles leaping off the roof of the camp on the lake in the country last summer. He was just seventeen at the time. Yet Charles was already several inches taller than me, and much more handsome. He was also a much better athlete. He had been born with the natural physical skill I always lacked. Charles had leapt with an easy confidence out into the summer air.

I smiled at the memory of his graceful leap as I staggered with hurting feet out of the bathroom. I got dressed in a black shirt and pants, pulled on my black sneakers, and headed into the city.

Coming out of the subway, I saw a neon sign across the way saying it was already ninety degrees. It seemed like I could feel the heat rising from the smelly pavements.

In the summer, the city never slept. As I waited for Crystal on the sidewalk of Ninety-third and Broadway a couple of drunks were wandering around, but I kept my head down and hid in the doorway of the store.

Again, I was struck by the incongruity of my life — ten years earlier, as a busy executive, at five in the morning I might have been riding the red-eye back from a trip to LA. Most summer mornings since being fired I would have been sleeping peacefully in our big old New England farmhouse, looking forward to a day of swimming and golf with my contemporaries who were already comfortably retired. Now I was standing in the dangerous dark of a sweaty New York City, waiting for my twenty-eight-year-old boss and scared that I might not be able to do good enough job of opening a

Starbucks store. My former entitled and arrogant self would have been appalled.

Crystal came up from the subway so well disguised I did not recognize her — in a black hood she fit my description of a tough street person to avoid that early in the morning.

I was relieved to see her, but she had no time for niceties. Brushing past me, she put her key in the door and told me to "lock it behind you."

I realized that every second would count and that we were off to the races. We had to open at 6 a.m. — just an hour to go.

"Give me a hand," Crystal said, and I helped her move the crates of pastries to the back. The pastries were delivered fresh each day to every Starbucks store.

"Here are the clean plates. Put the pastries on them. There's a schematic on the pastry case, telling you what goes where. I've got to get the coffee going."

As I moved to open the first pastry packages, Crystal suddenly yelled, "Stop!" and I jumped. I had never heard Crystal yell before.

"Put on some of these plastic gloves," Crystal said, handing me some. "We've got to be careful with food. Never touch the

171

pastries with your bare hands. Okay, get going."

I put on my green apron, taking a quick
look at the schedule that was always posted
on the bulletin board. Bianca was due in by
6:30 and then Joann would be in at 9:00.
Joann never came in too early, or stayed too
late. She had a child to take care of, and
since she was such a dedicated and compe-
tent worker, Crystal always gave her the
times she needed on the schedule. I was
glad to see that Bianca and Joann would be
coming in to help us with the morning rush.

Soon the store was filled with the aroma
of the delicious coffee that Crystal was
brewing. Crystal called to me as she did her
different opening steps, helping me learn as
she went through the process:

"I brew up today's coffee — Verona," she
called, "then I also brew up a batch of mild
coffee: Today it's Colombia. Finally I brew
some Decaf . . . right now I am brewing
Decaf Sumatra."

I nodded my head as she called these
specifics out to me. How did she think I
had time to learn?! I was doing the pastries
as quickly as possible before the store
opened. There were a lot of pastries — and
very little time.

I ripped open the plastic packages containing the scones. There were four different kinds of scones: blueberry, raspberry, cinnamon, and maple. There were five different varieties of muffins: bran, chocolate, corn cheddar, blueberry, and reduced fat blueberry. While there were just three different donuts — glazed, chocolate, and cinnamon — Starbucks served a variety of cakes: reduced fat blueberry cake, reduced fat cinnamon swirl, crumb cake, classic coffee cake, glazed lemon loaf, blueberry loaf, and banana nut loaf. I opened one chocolate croissant and one butter croissant. Then there were chocolate and oatmeal cookies, marshmallow crispy squares, espresso brownies, and a variety of others that had to be unwrapped and set up for later.

I looked at the visual display posted on the case that showed where each "a.m. pastry" should go. This was not like handling a register and trying to make change. I was confident that I would place the pastries exactly in their right positions — after a quick glance, the schematic was clear in my mind. I only had to look at it once or twice to keep it in my mind. At Yale, I had built up a good visual memory as a History of Art major who had to spend many a late night memorizing pictures. I smiled to think that my fancy college education was being put to use now — forty years later.

Until I hit the bagel packages. The bagels were tricky to get out. The packages were clearly designed to keep the bagels as fresh as possible, but they made it very hard to release them from the plastic coverings. It occurred to me that American civilization might be remembered for creating the most difficult-to-open plastic packages in the history of the world — all to keep things nice and antiseptic. But I had no time for such abstract thoughts as Crystal came to my rescue with a scissors. Perhaps I wasn't the only one who had a problem with the bagel bags.

As I cut the cinnamon raisin, sesame, and plain bagel bags open and finished placing out all the pastries, Crystal called out to me in instruction, "Now I'm making the iced tea. Passion, Black Iced Tea, Green Tea." I glanced at her to let her know I had registered her lesson.

"Now do the titles," Crystal said, handing me a small case containing little title cards for each pastry.

Once again, this effort was something I could do with relative ease. I was proud of myself as I matched up all the pastries correctly.

But there was more to do, and the clock

was ticking.

"I'm going to get the espresso bar open," Crystal said, "and you do the sandwiches."

The sandwiches went in the front of the pastry case. I ran around and put the egg salad, the tuna, and the turkey — all the various sandwiches — in the spots that were already marked in the case. While math was something I had never mastered, filling the cases according to a detailed visual was something I could do, and do easily.

I stood when I finished, observing the fully stocked case like it was indeed a work of art.

Crystal smiled at me.

"Good job, Mike," she said, and I felt like I had just won the Derby.

Our race was almost over. We had just about run out of time. It was just five minutes until six o'clock.

"Now assign yourself a register in the middle," Crystal said. I got a drawer from the middle register, weighed it out on the magical counting machine to $150 dollars, and put it back in my register just as I saw the first Guest waiting at the door.

"Open the door, Mike," Crystal called, busy getting the espresso bar ready, steaming the wands, and pulling a first "test" espresso drink to make sure everything was working right.

I went over and unlocked the door. We were open for business.

"Good morning," our first Guest said.

"Good morning," I said back, racing to get behind my register so I could ring him up.

"A Tall Skim Cappuccino," he told me, "and a plain bagel with jelly."

"A Tall Skim Cappuccino," I called to Crystal, and she called back to me: "A Tall Skim Cappuccino."

It was up to the Partners on the register to get the Guests their pastries, so I got out a bagel for him.

He handed me a five-dollar bill, and I made his change.

I remembered Crystal's telling me to make eye contact and conversation. I was a little less worried about screwing up on the cash register by now, so I decided to focus on what I knew I could do. After all, during my twenty-five years as an executive vice president at J. Walter Thompson I had been paid extremely well to talk — making conversation was not a problem for me.

"A Red Sox fan?" I asked the Guest, who was wearing a Sox cap. "I don't see that many here in New York."

"Actually, no," he laughed. As I made eye

contact, I noticed he had white hair and blue eyes, and an easy smile. "My roommate at Harvard Medical School was a rabid Red Sox fan. Over the last decades I have rooted for the Yanks, and he for the Red Sox. And the Yanks have won — every year. But since it's my sixtieth birthday this year, and he gave me this Red Sox hat, I promised him I would half root for the Sox."

"Half root?" I said, and he laughed.

"I wear the hat he gave me. That's as much as he gets."

He made his way over to a small table in the corner.

The next Guest in line was a young guy with a child that could not have been more than two years old, in a stroller. In my pre-Starbucks life, I would have pegged him as the type of guy who was too young and too irresponsible for a child, though it was clear to me today that this wasn't the case at all.

I greeted him. "Good morning."

"I'll have a Venti Latte, and a plain bagel for Ella."

"Ella?"

"My daughter, named after Ella Fitzgerald."

"Venti Latte," I called down the bar.

"Venti Latte," Crystal called back to me.

"You're a good father," I told him as I

made his change.

"I have to be," he said. "That's the deal I made with my wife. I take Ella out early. It gives my wife a few extra minutes to sleep."

"Great," I said as he pushed the stroller over to a table near the door. I liked the idea that our Starbucks store was a place he would find comfortable spending time with his little daughter so early in the morning.

I looked up to see a woman wearing a very pretty scarf and a beret. She had dark eyes and a big smile.

"One Venti Coffee . . . but what are you serving today?" she asked.

I looked behind me. We had a different coffee every week, but each was listed on the board.

"Verona," I said. "It's really good."

"I'll have a Venti of that. With a little room for milk."

I gave her the coffee, with room — register Partners also got the non-espresso drinks — and made her change.

"Thank you," she said. "The perfect way to start my day."

"Are you in the arts?" I guessed. There was something about her that seemed so artistic.

"Right the first time." She smiled. "My name is Denise. You'll see me here first thing each morning."

She turned and headed out the door. Denise was in the arts, but she was clearly a hardworking, disciplined person.

When the next Guest, a young mother with a child in her arms, brightly ordered, "A Two Pump Grande Decaf Skim No Whip Mocha," I repeated the drink down to Crystal: "A Two Pump Grande Decaf Skim No Whip Mocha."

Crystal called it back to me in a different order. "Decaf Grande Skim Two Pump No Whip Mocha." I knew you were supposed to call out the ingredients as they were listed on the cup, in order of importance. Obviously, Decaf was more important than the number of shots of Mocha.

The young woman noticed Crystal's correction and was grateful. "I have to have Decaf for now," she explained. "I'm pregnant . . . again."

I was impressed. "Well, it's great you got up so early, and got her dressed and —"

"My child is a *boy*. . . . His name is Max. My name is Rachel."

Suddenly I remembered that Rachel had introduced herself to me before, and had explained about her need for decaf. How stupid I was. I used to pride myself on my recall of names, but at the register, under stress, I was losing it.

"It's great you got Max dressed and out so early . . ." I stumbled out the response.

Rachel smiled at me.

"This is *not* voluntary," she said, explaining to me as though I were just a child myself. "I have to have my Mocha in the morning or I am not a good mother or good for anything!" She laughed and moved away, juggling her child and her hot Mocha with a dexterity that showed she had done it many times before.

Not voluntary, I thought to myself. *What a* great *business.* Starbucks was not something people decided for or against in a casual way. It was obviously a key part of their lives, an important destination for them every single day. Maybe even several times a day!

My mood had lifted so much since starting this job. And it occurred to me why: My old job involved sitting as a customer in Starbucks unable to find customers of my own. What a relief to me to have customers eager to greet me rather than my calling for clients like I had done in my own old business, and no one wanting to take my calls. I loved greeting these early morning Guests, and serving them. They probably had no idea what a gift it was simply to have them

180

waiting eagerly in line to see me.

"Hey, Mike," Crystal called over to me from her station at the espresso bar, in what I took to be a cheerful tone. "You are a natural."

"A natural?" I asked her.

"You are doing a great job at connecting this morning."

"Connecting?"

"With the Guests. A lot of Partners just make change, you make *conversation.* And you're funny. You are a funny guy!"

I thought she meant this as a compliment. Maybe I had shown her some confidence and competence that she had not expected. I felt the pride of a schoolkid whose teacher has praised him.

Crystal laughed as she turned back to her espresso machine.

What was so funny?

Was funny good? Over my many years of working in Corporate America, I had picked up the meaning of a plethora of business cues; all of these went out the window in dealing with Crystal.

The Guests and I did seem to be having some laughs as we talked. I was certainly having an enjoyable time, and they seemed to be as well.

When there was a break from the constant

stream of Guests, Crystal called over and casually but pointedly asked, "Who was that young girl I saw you with the other night?"

"My daughter."

Crystal gave me a surprised look and a smile. "Good for you," she said. It seemed to me there was a new kindness in her voice I hadn't heard before.

I had no more time to think about it.

"Iced Venti Americano, light on the ice," the next man told me, dressed for business with a pin-striped suit.

I realized there was a real mix of professions here on the Upper West Side. I liked that. No only did Starbucks have diversity in Partners, they also had diversity in Guests.

I looked up to see a line out the door. The more Guests in line, the less conversation I could have. Nonetheless, it seemed that a sea of positive energy was coming my way. Instead of being upset at seeing a new face in their morning routine, they were very welcoming to me.

In my haste to serve the next customer, I gave six dollars instead of sixteen dollars back to a professional-looking young woman carrying a computer in a case over her shoulder.

"I'm so sorry," I said. "I know you need

to get to work."

"Don't worry," she took the time to tell me before hurrying off. "You'll do great."

Crystal had talked to me about respect, but now I felt it not only from the Partners but also from the Guests.

How different this was from my job in the macho competitive world of J. Walter Thompson! The clients there often enjoyed a good laugh, but it usually came at my expense. Working on the Ford account, the client would sometimes get a positive pleasure when things went wrong. I recalled my first presentation to a bunch of New England Ford dealers. In my nervousness, as I got to my feet to make my presentation, I upset a pot of coffee, spilling it in the lap of Jerry Mantoni from Rhode Island. He was a multimillionaire car dealer. He leapt up, brushing off his shiny blue pants. I thought I would be fired for causing pain to such an important man, but the whole room of tough car dealers erupted in laughter. And then the dealers bought all my ideas. They told my boss they *always* wanted me at their meetings.

Another tense time, after presenting over two hundred new layouts of possible ads to Lee Iacocca — each layout representing many hours of extreme effort — he simply said: "Nothing here bites my ass." Once again the room erupted in laughter. Everyone at Ford lived in fear and loved to see someone else get publicly humiliated.

My first boss at J. Walter Thompson had told me, "Fear is a great motivator."

The ad you were working on was either great or a piece of shit. The game was win or lose. And it wasn't just the ad, but the person presenting the ad, that took the hit. You were either a great creative genius or a stupid piece of shit. If you won new clients, you were a hero; if you couldn't get any new clients, you were a bum. There was no in-between. And there certainly wasn't respect or dignity. Those words were literally never mentioned.

Here at Starbucks both the Partners and the Guests seemed to agree tacitly that everyone should be treated with respect and dignity. I had never seen any work environment like it. The best Fortune 500 companies I had encountered, despite spending months and lots of money writing and publishing high-sounding mission statements, never practiced the corporate gobbledygook they preached.

Bianca arrived at 6:30 on the dot. She gave me a sweet smile as she stepped up to her register. Bianca was small, and I guessed she wasn't older than nineteen, but she was much better than me at making change and calling drinks. I was grateful to have her by my side.

By the time Joann arrived at nine, the store was full to overflowing.

The three of us worked the registers while Crystal continued to make the espresso drinks at the bar. She never seemed to get flustered; despite the unending line and now all three of us calling out drinks to her. We were a coffee choir. "Iced Venti Skim Latte, Decaf Tall White Mocha, Grande Breva Vanilla Latte, Double Tall Cappuccino," we called, in our own sort of caffeinated three-part harmony.

"Take a ten," Crystal called to me at one point. After every couple of hours on the shift you were allowed to take a break. I was grateful to get out of the front lines for a while, and started toward the back room.

"Hey, Mike," Joann called. "Any broken pastries today?"

"I don't know," I answered. I had been so busy setting them out, I hadn't bothered to check for any damage.

"Go help him check the form," Crystal told her.

Joann moved toward me, and together we went to the back.

"When you put out the pastries, you always have to check for any damaged stuff. Then we can call them in to corporate, and get credit for 'em."

Joann spoke in a soft, soothing voice. I loved the way she instructed me . . . so gently.

She pulled out a pair of glasses and put them on.

"New glasses?" I said.

"Yeah, now I can see!" She laughed.

"You were faking it before?" I laughed along with her, not really believing it.

"Sort of," Joann said. "Never could see quite right, but hadn't been to any eye doctor. You know" — she looked at me with a smile — "Starbucks paid for my eye test *and* my glasses."

"Great," I said, meaning it. Free visual care had never been part of any benefits package for me — even with my big corporate job. Starbucks's benefits, especially considering Joann was just a part-time employee, were really unusual. In fact, I had never heard of anything like that before.

"You know Yvette?" Joann asked. Yvette was a new hire. She was going to school on the side. I had hardly seen her, and had not yet had a chance to work a shift with her. She was a tall African-American lady who always seemed in a big hurry.

"Yvette's not here today," Joann said. "Got to get her wisdom teeth out. That girl had never been to the dentist before."

I was dumbfounded. Never been to a dentist, and yet already going to college. I had a realization that Starbucks was giving people not only unique health benefits, but also encouragement to make sure they took care of themselves.

"Now," Joann continued, "did you see any checklist with those pastries you unpacked?"

"I didn't notice anything."

"You were probably hurrying too much," Joann said, looking around. Then she looked in the garbage can I had used to throw all the paper away. She came up with a typed list of pastries on a long sheet of paper.

She adjusted her new glasses.

"Let's check this," she said, taking out a pen. We went through all the pastries, making sure they were all right. There was one damaged raspberry scone.

"Let's share this," Joann said, smiling.

I was to discover that every Partner had their favorite pastries. Joann loved raspberry and blueberry scones. Bianca had a taste for the espresso brownies. Crystal's favorite was the toffee almond bar. It was hard for me to resist a chocolate chip cookie.

187

"Mike, would you mind coming back out?" I heard Crystal call from the front. I rushed back out to help at the registers.

Around ten, Kester came in to relieve Crystal. He gave me a big smile and really handled the bar in an equally magical way. Like Crystal he seemed to have no problem making the different combinations of the eighteen drinks. He still stayed relaxed as he called out, "Venti Extra Dry Cappuccino, Double Tall Latte, Grande Sugar Free Vanilla Skim Latte, Decaf Tall Caramel Machiatto, Tall No Whip White Mocha," and all the other different Lattes, Cappuccinos, Doppios, and Macchiatos. Then, as the morning wore on, and younger Guests appeared, there were calls for Caramel, Coffee, Mocha, and all the other different varieties of iced Frappuccinos that were a big favorite in the summer.

I took my half-hour meal break — it felt like five minutes — and then I was back on my feet working hard until my shift was done early that afternoon. I pulled off my green apron and made my way down to the basement to drop it in the dirty laundry. I had survived my first opening. It made the running of the bulls seem like a piece of cake.

In addition to being the place where

laundry and garbage were collected to be picked up later in the night, the basement was also a private space where people went when they wanted to be alone for a few minutes.

As I came down the stairs, I noticed that Crystal was over in the corner, talking on her cell phone. I didn't want to disturb her, but I had to walk past her to throw my apron in the laundry bag.

She closed her cell phone, shook her head, and passed her hand through her black hair. I couldn't help but notice she was crying.

I didn't want to intrude, but I also couldn't just be silent in the face of her distress. "What's the matter?"

Crystal sighed. "It's Winston. My cousin. He's had to go to the emergency room. . . . They think it might be his heart."

"That's bad," I said stupidly. My comment made Crystal look even more distressed. I wanted to help. I had an idea. Dr. Cohen was a real pain in the ass to me, always trying to get me to exercise more. He was a nut about preventive medicine. But in this case his tough love attitude might be perfect. He would know how to get the truth out of the people in the emergency room. He would know what to do.

"Why don't I call my doctor? He's a pain, but he really knows his stuff, and maybe he can help your cousin."

"Winston is overweight . . . always has been. He has high blood pressure. . . . Don't bother your doctor, there's plenty of doctors at the hospital."

"But this guy is really good at cutting through the nonsense some hospitals talk." I couldn't say it any other way. "He'll find out fast what's really wrong, and do something about it."

"Okay," Crystal said reluctantly.

I dialed Dr. Cohen's office number.

His assistant answered.

"Moira, this is Michael Gill. Is Dr. Cohen in?"

"He's on vacation."

"Vacation?"

"Mr. Gill, this is August."

"Okay, yeah. . . . Where is he?"

"At home."

"Where?"

"In his apartment in the city. You know how he hates to leave town."

"Moira, could you do me a big favor and give me his home number?"

"Just ask Information. He's listed. On Park Avenue."

I got his number.

Dr. Cohen answered on the first ring. "Hello."

"Hello. Doctor, I'm sorry to bother you —"

"Who is this?"

"Michael Gill . . ."

"How's the exercise going? Are you doing the stretching exercises I gave you every morning? Did you break something?"

"No, I'm calling for a friend. A cousin of hers just got taken to an emergency room and it would be really helpful if you could just give them a call and find out what is happening to him."

"August is the worst time to go to an emergency room in New York City. What's his name?"

"Winston?"

I looked over at Crystal.

"Winston Grove," she said. "He's at Mount Sinai."

I repeated the name to Dr. Cohen.

"That can be a real zoo," Dr. Cohen said. "Okay, it's not that far from my apartment. I'll walk over. Give me the number of your friend."

I gave him Crystal's cell number. The manager of each Starbucks store always gives her cell number to all the Partners, in case of emergency.

"Do your exercises," Dr. Cohen told me, and then hung up. I felt a surge of gratitude toward my doctor.

Crystal looked at me, wiping away the tears, not hoping for anything. (Later, I learned that Dr. Cohen had helped sort things out. It turned out that Winston did have high blood pressure, and some slight heart palpitations, but Dr. Cohen told Crystal if he went on a diet and got some exercise he would be okay.)

"Thanks, Mike," Crystal said, after I finished my phone call. "See you later. I want to go see Winston for myself."

She headed up the basement stairs, and then she stuck her head back down.

I turned to look back up at her.

"You did good on the opening," she said, and then she was gone.

6
THE
MILLION-DOLLAR
PUNCH

"Try a little tenderness . . ."
— lyric by Otis Redding, played during a
closing at Starbucks

September–October

More than a month passed, and I began to
get into a more confident state about Starbucks. Handling the opening of the store
with Crystal had been a big breakthrough
for me, and I was getting more used to calling out drinks and making conversation at
the same time — although I still made a lot
of mistakes. Then one day, when she was
making up the schedule for next week,
Crystal told me: "It's time you closed,
Mike."

She could see by my expression that I was
worried. I had still not lost the habit of fear-
ing any new challenge.

"Don't worry," Crystal continued. "You'll
be closing with Kester. He's the best in the

business."

Fall seemed to have come earlier than ever this year, the days growing shorter. I shivered a little as I waited for my train. Partly from the cold, but also from the fact I was going to check on my tumor. I was not due into work until 8:30 that evening, so I had decided to use the day to go in to have another MRI. Dr. Lalwani's assistant had called several times to make sure I would schedule an appointment. She had become more and more insistent. It had been more than six months since I had seen him and heard the shocking news that there was a "small growth" at the bottom of my brain.

I had told my children about the tumor — emphasizing that it was not *terminal* and *nothing* had to be done right away. Still, I knew they were concerned.

I had *not* told Crystal or my other Partners about my tumor. I didn't want them to pity me. My growing confidence and enjoyment of working with them was based in part on the fact that my Partners gave me no quarter and did not make any special allowances for me — despite the fact that I was so much older. I had, I realized now, been deferred to all my adult life, and did I not want any more of that special status. Once, at JWT, they had done an interview with everyone who worked for me. I was surprised when people said they were afraid of me. I thought of myself as a "benevolent dictator." Obviously my employees didn't find me so benevolent as a boss.

Now, my Partners didn't care about my background or my age or my education or my ability to create "successful selling ideas." During a shift at Starbucks there was such pressure that it was a kind of *immediate democracy* — no time for anything but equality of opportunity to get the job done, done right, and done quickly. You had to grab that Tall Coffee With Room with speed, and cooperate with your Partners, or the whole experience wouldn't work for everyone. I loved that feeling of being just one more part of a well-functioning team — no special treatment for me.

I had also felt that if I told my Partners about my tumor, and how it made it hard for me to hear in one ear, they would be, naturally, sympathetic, and try to compensate for me. Or, even worse, when I was still proving myself as I was each day, they would doubt my ability to help them. I was sure they wouldn't say anything directly, but I could imagine that such doubt would undermine their confidence in me. That was certainly the way I would react if a Partner told me he or she had a hearing problem. *Hearing* was such an essential part of the whole experience. And I had been proud that despite my diminished hearing I was able to call and re-call the drinks as well as anyone, and make conversation at the register without missing a beat. On the other hand, I also recognized that I missed some things when the music was loud and the Frappuccino machine was crushing the ice. I made an extra effort to concentrate and get all the orders correct.

One final reason I didn't want to tell my Partners about my tumor was that I didn't want to think about it *myself.* Sometimes at night before I got to sleep I would hear the buzzing in my left ear. I hated the fact that somehow I had, out of all the millions of people, been given this rare and constant affliction. Yet I was also grateful that it was not worse: I could be dead, or dying. My daughter Bis had given me a Bose radio, and I played classical music, which helped the buzz to go away so I could sleep.

Now I hoped I could postpone the dreaded operation once again.

Dr. Lalwani's assistant had set up the MRI and a meeting with the doctor afterward so that it could all be done in the space of a couple of hours. The MRI was painless, but I waited in a kind of suspended agony outside Dr. Lalwani's office afterward. At one point he came out and saw me there. He probably also saw the painful expression on my face and my foot tapping nervously on the floor.

"Go down the hall and get an ear exam," he told me.

Dutifully, I went down the hall.

They say doctors are like gods. He had my fate in his hands. I was going to be as obedient as I could.

"Dr. Lalwani sent me for an ear exam," I told the lady at the desk.

They gave me one immediately. Clearly his name was magic in this hospital. I thought of the old joke: "I'm dying of cancer, but I've got the greatest doctor in America."

I tried every way to fool the person giving me the ear exam, yelling out a firm "yes!" when I couldn't hear a thing, but she ended up saying that my hearing was just 20 percent in my left ear.

"But my right ear is perfect!" I said, helping to put a positive spin on it. Putting a positive spin on things had been my profession. And my parents had always encouraged me to be positive about everything —

a cheerleader for them, as though they were the children and I was the parent egging them on.

"Not perfect," the young woman had replied, checking the chart, unfazed by my attempt at optimism, "but normal for your age."

"Normal for my age." I hated those words. Starbucks had given me an increasing confidence that I could almost keep up with people a generation or two younger, and here she was bringing me back to the dreaded fact that I was three score and four years old.

I shuffled — like a shuffleboard player — down the corridor, carrying my ear test results back to Dr. Lalwani.

He ushered me into his inner office immediately.

He was smiling. But then, I had come to realize that Dr. Lalwani was always smiling. He had smiled when he gave me the shocking news that I had a rare tumor at the base of my brain. Was it his inner happiness or a nervous tick . . . or did, I hoped against hope, his smile *this* time indicate some confidence about these specific results of my MRI?

"Good news," he said, slapping the MRI up on his light machine that was mounted on the wall of his office. "The tumor has hardly grown at all."

"What does that mean?"

"The smaller the tumor the more elegant the operation can be."

"Elegant."

"Let's just say a smaller tumor makes things easier."

"But you still have to cut into my head?"

"Yes."

"And you said it was serious."

"Any brain operation is serious."

He was still smiling. I realized Dr. Lalwani was one of those people that *are* in a state of happiness. He had clearly followed his bliss. It was just a kind of crazy occurrence that his bliss was opening people's skulls.

"But if it" — I couldn't say tumor — "hasn't grown a lot, maybe I don't need the operation right now."

Dr. Lalwani looked at my MRI again.

"Correct," he said slowly. "We could continue for another few months of watchful waiting."

I had heard the term "watchful waiting" before. It had sounded like a bad news prescription. Now I loved the sound of that medical cliché, and grabbed at the tired phrase like a drowning person reaches for *any* support.

"Sounds good," I said. I wanted to say, *Sounds great!* but didn't want to appear too enthusiastic. I didn't want Dr. Lalwani to realize that I would do almost anything to avoid going under his knife.

"And your hearing has not degenerated significantly," he said, more to himself than me, looking at my audio tests.

"No, no," I leapt in. "Not degenerated at all. I am able to keep up with all the complicated orders at Starbucks."

"Starbucks?" I had forgotten I had not mentioned my job to him. He knew so little about me. To Dr. Lalwani, I was clearly just another candidate for a successful operation.

"What do you do there?" he said, beginning to gather up my MRI and get ready for the next patient. "Manage a store?"

"No, I just work there."

He looked at me. The idea didn't make sense to him, but he obviously didn't have time to figure it out.

"Okay," he said, focusing again on me as a patient, not a Starbucks Partner, "I will have Lisa call you and set up another MRI in a few months."

I got up quickly and shook his hand.

Isn't it amazing in life how one minute

you are devastated by some news, but then, a few seconds later, your desperate need to survive at any price kicks in and you can find some way to turn it around in your head? I had heard that I wasn't going to have a major operation for a least a little while, and I was *relieved*. Almost, I had to admit, pleased!

I left his office in a hurry, not wanting him to change his mind. I had a fear of hospitals and operations. Also, I knew that if I had to leave my job at Starbucks at this point, it would be hard on me, and hard on my Partners as well. I was just beginning to understand how to help.

I hadn't even had a chance to close yet!

It was already dark when I got the store . . . past eight o'clock. My shift was to be 8:30 until half past midnight.

Kester was there and greeted me with a big smile. Crystal was in the back, but on her way out she pulled me aside.

"Sometimes there's trouble with Guests during closing times," she said, in her professional, no-nonsense voice. "Whatever you do, don't touch a Guest."

"Touch a Guest?" I was surprised, and a little disturbed. What did she mean?

"I'm talking about getting someone to leave, even taking their arm. A Partner here

hit a Guest once who wouldn't leave. . . .
We got sued for a million dollars, and I had
to fire him. No million-dollar punches."

I almost laughed. Didn't she know whom
she was talking to? A congenital coward.

But I just said, "I promise. No punches."

I thought with a smile back to the one and
only fight experience of my life.

"What's so funny?" Crystal asked, seeing
me smile.

"Nothing," I said. "I was just remembering seeing Muhammad Ali."

"You saw Ali?" Kester came over to join
the conversation.

"Yeah, I saw his *first professional* fight in
New York, against Doug Jones."

"Cool," Kester said.

"Doug Jones was his first fight after winning a gold at the Olympics. He fought right
here in New York. At Madison Square Garden."

"Listen," Crystal interrupted, clearly not
interested in hearing my fight talk with
Kester, "just be careful, Mike. Okay?"

Crystal was in her professional mode. She
had an important point to make and didn't
want me to treat it casually.

I looked at her without a smile.

"Got it," I said.

"See ya." She headed out the door. Tonight there was a different fancy black car waiting for her.

"Who's that?" I asked Kester.

"Crystal's ride. She goes first class." Kester smiled, and then he called: "Hey, Charlie, come on over. Mike's got a story about Muhammad Ali."

Charlie pulled off his earphones and joined us. Fortunately, there were no Guests waiting to be served.

"Ali's first professional fight," I said, "just blocks from here, down at the old Madison Square Garden. He won in ten rounds."

I could see by the expectant looks on their faces they wanted more. They had probably not even been born when Ali was fighting.

"Ali said that he could 'float like a butterfly, sting like a bee.' "

"Cool," Charlie said. "That almost sounds like rap." Charlie was into music, and everything to him probably sounded like a possible rap song.

"Sort of," I said. "Ali was definitely a *poet.*"

"How so?" Charlie said, and Kester also gave me a quizzical look.

"He'd make up poems about his fights. He made up one for me. I was working for a magazine and I asked for a poem, and in the locker room Ali just made one up."

"The guy was good," Charlie said, and Kester nodded. "Just making up a quick verse."

I realized that Charlie was impressed by Ali's word skill.

I did not tell them that I had forced my way into Ali's locker room by saying I was "press" and that I had asked him for a poem in my position as editor of the *Yale Literary Magazine.* They weren't interested in how I had met Ali. They wanted to hear about *him.* I did share the poem that Ali had created.

" 'Old Doug Jones was fat as a hen . . . ,' Ali said."

Kester and Charlie started to laugh.

" 'But he fooled me, he lasted ten.' "

"That's pretty good," Charlie, said. "Not bad for right off the top," and he gestured toward his head.

"He was the fastest, smartest boxer ever," I said, still trying to convey how amazing it was to the whole world to have such a great person who was also such a great athlete with such uncanny verbal ability that he could just sit down with a towel around his waist, after the biggest fight of his life so far, and knock off a little verse for some guy he had never met before.

They had liked to hear about Ali, but time on any Starbucks shift is very limited —

there was always work to do.

Charlie put his earphones back in, listening to his own CD, while he started to clean up the espresso bar, and Kester said: "Mike, would you like do the front of the store?"

"Sure," I said.

"Here, let me get you started. It all starts with a *mop.* You've got to get your mop and water ready."

We went to the back room. Kester gave me a mop and showed me how to fill up the pail with hot water and special soap that cleaned the floor with efficacy but dried relatively quickly.

"Now you are ready," he said, helping me push the mop and pail back to the front of the store. The pail was on little wheels, so it rolled right along.

"First you sweep," Kester said, pausing once we were in front of the counter. "Keep sweeping all night, so there's not that much to do in the last hour. Also, your job will be to make sure the condiment bar has all the napkins, sugar, and everything is just right. So keep that stocked. And the bean wall. People will buy pounds of different coffees tonight. You replace them. When the shift opens in the morning, and you know what that is like, there's no time to restock the coffee. Since every second counts when you open, we've got to make sure tonight we've got everything we can ready to go for the first shift."

Kester paused. This was already the longest I had heard him talk about anything. But he clearly had thought through the responsibilities of closing. I had heard the other Partners talk about Kester as a "great closer." I was happy to be learning from the best.

"We can't make the coffee for the morning," Kester continued, gesturing toward the espresso bar and the coffee urns, "but we can make sure all the coffee beans are fully stocked. Right now you can take out the garbage. Just get it from the basement and put it outside by the curb. They'll pick it up later."

Kester gave me a hit on the back, encouraging me. He never seemed to doubt that I could do what he asked me to. It meant something to me that he seemed to treat me almost as though I were just another guy his age.

But the garbage was a physical challenge for me. There were probably twenty garbage bags full of coffee grounds and other stuff. They were very heavy. And I had to climb a steep iron stairway. I could feel my heart pounding as I lifted them up the almost vertical incline, and I started to sweat. I told myself this was good for me: a form of aerobic exercise. I tried to smile, although it was more of a grimace with the strain of carrying the heavy bags.

I struggled with the huge load of heavy garbage bags and was about halfway up the stairs when I almost ran into Charlie on his way down. He had his earphones on and was rocking to music, but he saw me in time and quickly backed up the stairs with a casual athletic grace that I envied. While I had never been an athlete, these young Partners made me realize that I was forty years older. I struggled with chores that they did so easily. I had seen Kester carry two heavy cases of vanilla syrup that had to weigh twenty pounds apiece up these same iron stairs — almost running. And now Charlie didn't miss a beat almost dancing back up the stairs I was having so much difficulty negotiating.

He took his earphones off as I passed him at the top, which I took as a mark of courtesy.

"Can I grab those?" he asked.

"Got it," I said defensively, though it was at heart a kind gesture. I was terrified I would be perceived as too old for any job. If closing the store meant carrying a bunch of heavy garbage bags up steep stairs, I wanted to prove I needed no help.

Charlie seemed not to notice. He started fiddling with his earphones, getting ready to put them back in again.

"Hey, Mike, you closing tonight?"

"Yeah."

"Cool," Charlie said. "Let's take it up a notch."

Charlie was always full of such upbeat energy. I had worked with him several times already. He would come in early and have a "red eye," a drink with one shot of espresso in regular coffee. He seemed to literally bounce through his shift, as though powered with extra caffeine.

Charlie had told me several weeks before that he was putting together a "music company." Almost every time I saw him he showed me a new CD he had made. The last one had featured a big picture of Charlie on the cover. He was a handsome young guy with a small mustache. In the photo he had his shirt open and a big gold cross on his chest.

"From my grandma," Charlie said. "Always wear it when I do my stuff."

He laughed, but I knew he was serious.

Beneath his cheerful jive, Charlie was a serious man. With big dreams.

Now he put the earphones back in, carefully making sure that they were in as far as possible, and then ran down the stairs. Ran! I kept moving forward, realizing in many ways in this job I was really out of my league.

I tried to hurry from the back of the store out to the curb with the heavy garbage bags; trying to make up the time I had lost struggling up the stairs.

As I got to the door, stooped to one side with the weight of the bag, it was opened for me by a Guest. I had noticed that many of our Guests treated Partners with extra courtesy. It was as if they wanted to make sure we weren't working too hard. Was this normal in most retail establishments? As a customer in the past, had I ever opened the door for employees while I shopped? Why did they do this? Was it something about the fact they were indulging themselves with an expensive drink of coffee? Did they feel a kind of guilt at the pleasure they were taking, and want to make sure we were not being abused?

Several times I had Guests stop me when I was cleaning off a table to ask, "How are they treating you?"

"Great," I replied truthfully. "Great people, great coffee . . . and great benefits."

The Guests always smiled when they heard this. Perhaps they wanted the whole Starbucks experience to be as positive for the people who were serving them as it was for them. I wasn't entirely sure. I had certainly never been treated with such genuine concern by any of my clients in twenty-five years of advertising. Even when I had my own little business, clients' inquiries would begin with a quick, perfunctory "How's it goin'?" to which they almost never wanted or expected a real answer before they got down to their business. They didn't really care. I sensed with the Starbucks' Guests, on the other hand, that they were genuinely concerned. If I or any other Partners had replied in the negative, I got the sense that they were ready to do battle on our behalf.

Whatever the reason, I was grateful to whomever was opening the door for me now as I was stumbling with three heavy bags of trash.

"Thanks," I said, glancing at his face.

He also looked at me.

"Michael Gates?"

He knew my first name and middle name. The name my family and old friends called me. My mother said when she called me "Michael" in Central Park, it was such a common name that a hundred kids ran up. So she started calling me Gatesy for short. My old friends often called me Michael or Gates or, sometimes, Michael Gates Gill. People, everyone, Partners and Guests, at Starbucks called me Mike. So this was someone from my previous life. I was embarrassed. During the last weeks I had tried to learn not only the drinks but also the names of the frequent Guests, but now I looked closer, pausing halfway out the door with my garbage bags.

"Benjamin?" I said.

"It *is* you!" he explained with pleasure. It was Benjamin Zucker, a friend I hadn't really seen since Yale. We had first met and bonded sharing a terrible, boring require-ment class during freshman year. Everyone had to take some "science" course, and Benjamin and I had ended up choosing the least evil alternative: a geology class taught by someone with the improbably appropri-ate name of Professor Flint. Naturally we called him "Rocky" Flint. The class was an agony for me. I knew I had to pass and write a long paper on the geology of the New Haven area. West Rock. East Rock. Rocks! Benjamin and I would spend long nights trying to fake it. We would write long sentences about strata and levels of granite

211

or, yes, flint, not knowing what made sense, but trying to sound scientific and making it all as obscure as possible. We hoped that if we made our sentences so complicated as to be almost incomprehensible the grader might forgive us, thinking we knew more than we could articulate.

Benjamin would laugh as we struggled to create something out of nothing. His laughter helped me endure.

For Benjamin seemed to take this deadly geology class with a light heart. In fact, he seemed to approach Yale with a relaxed spirit I could not match. I was weighed down with the generations of my family who had preceded me at Yale. I could not afford to fail. Benjamin didn't even seem to consider that possibility.

Benjamin was the first of his family to go to Yale, or any school in America. For him it was all a great adventure.

Now I found myself, three garbage bags in hand, forty-two years later, meeting him again.

"I can't believe you are here," Benjamin started, and then he surprised me by finishing, "this is my neighborhood Starbucks!"

I had fully expected him to say that he could not believe I was working at Starbucks, carrying garbage. Instead, he was apparently delighted I was working so close to his home.

"I live just blocks away," Benjamin continued.

"Great," I said. "Just a minute."

I completed my task of taking the garbage bags out to the street.

Out of the corner of my eye, I saw Kester watching me. He always seemed to make sure I was doing the right thing, and I decided I had better introduce my old, new-found friend.

"Kester, this is Benjamin, an old friend."

Kester looked surprised. It occurred to me that it might be hard for him to imagine that this guy, a well-dressed Guest from the neighborhood, was an old friend of mine. To Kester, I expected, I was just an old guy down on my luck. Benjamin seemed so prosperous and positive — someone who didn't belong in my world.

Benjamin also looked ten years younger than I did, so maybe that threw him off.

"Cool" was all Kester said.

"I'm working right now," I said to Benjamin, getting ready to head back to the basement. "I'm afraid I'm not going to be able to talk right now."

"When do you get off?" Benjamin was not to be brushed aside that easily.

"Not until after midnight."

"Okay, so we'll meet some other time. I come in here a lot."

"Would you like a coffee?" I asked, trying not to be rude. Why should I treat Benjamin worse than any other Guest? Because I was embarrassed, that's why!

"Venti Latte," Benjamin said.

He seemed so at ease with the whole situation. I found it awkward. Kester started to make his drink.

"Here's my number," Benjamin said, handing me a big business card. "Call me. We'll have a Latte."

I turned to go.

"This is so great," Benjamin said as I turned to head back downstairs. "I just live two minutes from here."

I appreciated the easy way Benjamin had taken to the idea of my working at Starbucks, and the positive way he greeted the discovery. The other former friends I had told about my job at Starbucks had reacted in two ways:

A kind of shocked silence, the way you might greet a person who told you he had cancer.

Or, even more painful to me, a kind of condescending encouragement — "Sounds good. I hear Starbucks is a great company.

Are you managing a store, or in marketing for them?"

"No, I just work as a barista, at the register, cleaning —"

"Sounds great," they would hasten to say, not wanting to hear the painful details.

Working at a low level at Starbucks was a sign I had fallen through the net that was supposed to support the white, upper-middle class. It was as though my disease of poverty were contagious. Most of my friends couldn't wait to get off the phone.

I headed down to the basement, leaving Benjamin talking with Kester. I remembered that, as well as writing well about a subject he did not know, Benjamin could talk to just about anyone about anything. He had been born in Nice, fled the Nazis, and his family barely made it out of Europe alive. But he seemed to view that horrific past as a great adventure. *What a gift,* I thought as I made my way back down those iron stairs, *to be able to take all that happened to you with such a lighthearted spirit, a genuine sense of humor about a mixed-up world.* At Yale he didn't even consider the fact that anyone could "fail" at life. Life was life — with all its bizarre twists and turns.

I realized I had spent most of my life trying not to fail. Trying to meet my parents' high expectations. Terrified of letting my family down. It had all been, I felt now, a terrible burden for me. And so stupid of me!

I picked up a few more garbage bags, and I headed back up the stairs. Reaching the front room, I was relieved to see that Benjamin was gone. I was no longer embarrassed about having my job. Yet I was worried that I had not become *good enough* at my job to be seen by people I knew. I wasn't confident enough to even invite my kids to see me work. And I was also still too concerned with what it all might look like.

When my trash duty was done, I stood back proudly and looked at the great pile of garbage bags I had built on the corner of Ninety-third and Broadway. I was surpised by the peculiar sense of satisfaction I felt at the hill I had created on the corner of the street.

I would try to laugh more, I told myself, hurrying back inside. There was a lot more to do! Over the sound system, Otis Redding was singing, "Try a little tenderness."

I promised myself I would try a little tenderness. Starting with myself. I would not be so hard on myself. What was the big deal? I was working, and working hard, and learning a job . . . like most of the rest of the world.

I was not Saint Michael. And I was not selfish Michael. I was just Mike, a guy who needed to survive, and I was grateful I had lucked out with such a job.

I swept the floor, once, twice, three, four times. Almost every time I swept, I found new things, like crumbs from pastries or dropped straws on the floor. We still had plenty of Guests, and I had to clean up after them.

I got obsessive about sweeping the floor, because I knew the clock was running. Kester would expect me to mop and clean when we shut the doors, and do it quickly. The cleaner the floor *before* I mopped, the better job I could do.

As it neared midnight, Kester came up to me. He put his hand on my shoulder. "Could you do me a favor, Mike?"

I was reminded again how much I liked that unique Starbucks style — not ordering someone around, but asking in a courteous way. When I was a big boss at J. Walter Thompson, I would come around late on a Friday and order people, "You have to work this weekend."

I never asked them or implied they were doing me a favor by working so hard. It was part of the macho code that you never explained, you just demanded immediate obedience.

Starbucks was so different.

"Sure," I said to Kester, eager to be of help.

As I was sweeping and re-sweeping during the night, the Otis Redding song was played and replayed on the Starbucks sound system. It was true to the spirit of the place. Starbucks seemed to have created a culture that tried to guide Partners with a kind of tenderness. It was a rare soft style to find in such a demanding retail business. Even Kester had acquired this gentle approach, now asking me to "do a favor" rather than giving me a direct order.

"Charlie and I will handle the registers and the espresso bar during the closing," Kester continued. "Could you clean the bathroom? Crystal says you are the best cleaner ever!"

He gave me his big smile.

I laughed.

"Can do!" I said, with a feeling of surprising pleasure.

I, Michael Gates Gill, was a good toilet cleaner. I couldn't yet make espresso drinks, I struggled carrying heavy garbage, and I still didn't feel good at the register, but I had confidence that I could make the bathroom sparkling clean. It was something I had done many times by now.

I gathered the mop and bucket, my broom, two different cleaners: one a disinfectant spray for the mirror and the garbage can in the bathroom, the other a heavy-duty cleaner for the toilet itself. Fully armed for the task, I approached the bathroom door. The little gizmo in the lock read: "Occupied."

I was annoyed. It was eleven-thirty already. People had been in and out of the bathroom all night. It was a big feature of the Starbucks welcome. But I needed to get in. Now. Once again, I heard the clock ticking. If I could do the bathroom right now, it was one less thing I would have to worry about in the last closing minutes. I was exhausted after being on my feet since since early that morning. (One of the problems I discovered with closing is that if you lived a normal life, you were often tired by the time you got to the store to start the late shift.)

I waited. Ten minutes went by. I restocked the bean wall, restocked the condiment bar, and swept once again, making sure to dig out every crumb from every corner. I checked my watch every minute, and then the door, but the "Occupied" sign remained. Finally, I banged on the door.

"Take it easy!" yelled a male voice from inside. Whatever he was doing, I was certain it wasn't going to be making the bathroom any easier for me to clean.

Nearly twenty minutes later the door finally opened. A kid came out carrying a computer and lugging a huge backpack. What was he doing in there?

On closer look, he wasn't a kid; he was just dressed like a kid. Unshaven, with long blond hair, he looked like a hippie, but his face was full of lines and his bright blue eyes shone with anger. He was a young man, yet old before his time. He smelled of cigarette smoke and other smells. I suspected he had been shooting up or using drugs while in the bathroom.

He looked at me like I was some kind of bug.

"Go for it," he said with a sarcastic smile, pushing past me and making his way over to a table in the corner.

At this point, few Guests remained in the store.

I rushed into the bathroom. It was a mess. Toilet paper everywhere. I blamed the young-old man for everything. I cleaned with a focused passion. I washed the mirror and sanitized the sink and toilet. I emptied the garbage in the bathroom and washed down the floor and the sides of the walls. I cleaned the door and sanitized the door handles. I replaced the toilet paper. It took me over twenty minutes, and I knew I was already short of time. I still had to check the condiment bar one last time to make sure there were enough sugars. We had five different kinds of sugar and they always needed to be replaced, which meant a time-consuming trip to the basement. I also could count on the fact that we needed fresh coffee packages for the bean wall, fresh napkins, and I still needed to clean the windows, the door, and the glass of the pastry case. The problem with the bathroom had cost me precious time that I could not afford to lose.

After finishing the bathroom, I asked Kester for the keys.

"What's up?" Kester asked. "We don't close for another half hour."

"I know, but I thought I'd shut the bathroom down now. I just cleaned it."

"Can't shut it until the store shuts. Mike, you are getting into this" — I thought he was going to say "shit" but he stopped himself in time — "cleaning stuff good, but don't go over the top! You'll do fine."

Kester had sensed my almost pathological impatience and, like a good coach, was trying to calm me down. "Stay cool. Once the last Guest leaves, you can go for it!"

My watch seemed to move so slowly as we got to the official closing time of 12:30.

Finally the dials aligned. I swept for the last time. All the Guests had gone but one.

My nemesis.

I walked up to his table. The guy who had brushed me off. Who had made fun of me and my eagerness to clean the bathroom.

He was deep into his computer.

He had unpacked his backpack and had papers scattered everywhere.

"We're closing," I told him, happy to have a reason to kick him out.

He didn't look at me and continued typing on his laptop.

"Sir," I said, struggling against every natural inclination to yell at him, "it's past twelve-thirty. We've got to close."

I even added a half-felt "Sorry."

He looked up at that.

"*You* sorry piece of shit, stop bothering me. I'm in the middle of something."

I stared at him.

His bright blue eyes stared straight at me, but seemed to look far beyond me.

He was scary.

As I had told Crystal, I was a coward, and had not fought anyone — ever.

"I'm sorry, sir, but you have to leave," I said. Though I was scared, his dismissive attitude had made my blood boil.

"Fuck you," he said, turning back to his computer screen.

I moved closer to him, remembering not to touch. I didn't even touch his backpack. But my move, as timid and timorous as it was, aroused something in him.

He slammed his computer case. In one fluid motion, he seemed to rise and pull something out from his back pocket. I had a quick thought: Was he going to pull out a wallet to try and buy me off?

But he wasn't about to try to bribe me to be nice. It wasn't a wallet. It was a knife, which he flicked open with practiced ease. I saw the glitter of the metal and stood transfixed.

I couldn't think. I was frozen. I gripped my mop, maybe with an unconscious desire to protect myself from him.

"One more fuckin' step," he said, his voice squeaking with rage, "and you are one dead fuckin' old man."

That really got to me. I hated anyone calling me old. Especially in this job. Especially now. I was challenged to keep up with the other Partners, and I was proud of the fact I had done so.

I took another step toward him and raised the handle of the mop. What was I going to do? Mop him to death?

Kester appeared from nowhere.

"Hey, Mike," he said, addressing me, "Charlie needs some help."

Kester didn't even look at the knife or the man holding it, but I could see the crazy guy look at him. Kester's size and strength were obvious. And the tone in Kester's deep voice was tough. I had never heard him speak to me like that . . . not that he said anything wrong, but he said it with a kind of cold finality. I turned to go, happy to have an out. My heart was racing.

Before I had taken more than a few steps away, I saw that the man was putting his knife away and picking up his stuff.

Kester silently watched him.

I went to get Charlie, who was moving fast to clean the espresso bar, dancing to some music he was creating in his head. By the time I got to tell Charlie about it, it was all over.

The guy was moving to the door, and Kester, right behind him like a big shadow, locked the door.

Neither Kester nor the guy had exchanged a single word.

I was shaken.

I asked Kester how he had known that I had needed help at that moment.

"I always got a feeling for when things go bad," Kester said. "Okay, get mopping. . . . Time to make your move, Mike."

Kester's voice was now relaxed again, and he gave me a smile of encouragement.

I went back and got my mop and bucket, and worked hard to get everything as clean as possible. The effort was a great relief to me because I didn't have time to think about what had happened. It wasn't easy to move all the tables and the chairs, mop the floor, mop it again to make sure it was clean, then put all the tables and chairs back. Wipe everything down one more time. Make sure the condiment bar and the bean wall were all stocked. I was sweating heavily when Kester called.

"Okay, Mike, let's go. There's a subway I got to catch."

I pulled off my apron and made my way downstairs.

Kester and Charlie were changing into their street clothes: do-rags, big caps, baggy pants, and boots. They were completely transformed from the smiling Partners in green aprons. They both had earphones dangling down their chests. When I went back upstairs, I was accompanied by two

225

guys who I would have at one point typed as hip-hop artists or gangsters — probably both. But now I knew when I saw guys like these, they might be something else too. They had lives and loves that were as full or fuller than mine. Yvette had once called Charlie "eye candy." Charlie always seemed to have a lot of girlfriends coming around to see him when he was working, and even many of the female Guests seemed to glow with a special brightness in Charlie's charismatic presence.

Even tonight, when I was sweeping, a woman had stopped me, gestured toward Charlie, who was busy at the bar, and said: "Can you get me his number?"

I had been told by Kester when I first started that you should *never* give out the phone numbers of Partners.

"Don't even tell 'em when they're supposed to be working," Kester had said. "You never know why someone is looking for someone."

So I felt in the right to say no to the woman.

A few minutes later, I went over to tell Charlie what I had done. He was busy dismantling each piece of the espresso bar, washing it, rinsing it, and putting it in the Sanitizer. The Sanitizer was like a dishwasher — just about twice as powerful and ten times as fast. As Charlie loaded this powerful machine, he moved with the agile grace that I envied. He hardly paused as I talked to him: "A girl wanted your phone number, but I told her no way."

Charlie gave me a quick, surprised look, still loading the Sanitizer.

"Kester told me we shouldn't give out numbers," I continued.

"Yeah, he might feel that way," Charlie said, laughing a little, slamming the door of the Sanitizer, "but, man, at least give me a chance to see for myself what I might be missing."

I felt bad as I went back to sweeping up the floor in front. I had made the wrong decision for Charlie. He could clearly handle a lot of female attention.

Although I *had* seen him several times in the last months locked in serious conversations with Kester in the basement before or after he started his shift, and I got the sense that Kester was trying to talk some sense into him. Kester was just twenty-three, Charlie nineteen, but somehow Kester seemed a lot more mature about life. Many of the younger Partners seemed to turn to Kester almost like a father figure, or a responsible uncle they had never had.

I don't mean that Kester was all business. I had met his girlfriend . . . a beautiful, quiet girl. Kester could laugh, we all laughed a lot with him at work, and I knew that Kester spent free time playing soccer, touch football, and other sports with his friends in Central Park on the weekends. Once, he had come in limping and Crystal had said: "You hurt yourself?"

"No," Kester had clearly lied.

"You've got to stop playing so hard," she said.

Kester laughed.

"Yes, Mama."

Crystal had the grace to laugh with him. She was like a tough-love mother to Kester . . . to all of us.

"Clock out," Kester told me, bringing me back to the present.

He and Charlie were moving fast. This whole night they'd been moving about twice as fast as me. I did not know the job as well as them, but I also had to admit to myself that I *was* old.

Kester made a quick tour of the store, including the bathroom, to make sure everything was in order for the morning shift.

After almost running back to the door, he locked it.

Then we all turned and ran down to the subway.

"The express leaves in five minutes. . . . If I miss it, I have to wait another half hour," Kester said.

I ran with my Partners down the subway stairs. Or, rather, they ran; I made my way down as quickly as I could, holding on to the rail on the side.

I was heading downtown to Times Square to catch the shuttle to Grand Central.

Kester and Charlie were heading up to One Hundred Twenty-fifth Street. But we stood together on the platform, waiting. I was breathing hard.

"Hey, Mike," Kester said, grabbing my shoulder, "you did a great job on the close."

I felt an unusual swell of pride.

The uptown subway roared into the station.

Kester and Charlie, now with their earphones on, got in.

My subway took another ten minutes to arrive.

In that time, I went over in my mind all that had happened tonight. I could have gotten in real trouble, I realized, despite Crystal's warning not to get in a confrontation with anyone. I promised myself I wouldn't let my anxiety to do a good job interfere with my judgment next time. Why had I gotten so pissed off at that backpack guy? Because I wanted to close . . . but maybe, just maybe, I had to admit to myself . . . I had gotten so angry with him because he hadn't respected me.

It was clear to me in that moment, as my subway finally slammed into the station, and I got on under the bright, unforgiving lights, that I had still not really internalized for myself the respect I felt for the other Partners and the job we all did. If they were worthy of respect, so was I.

I was still too proud, and prideful . . . too quick to take offense. The backpack guy had been wrong, but I had encouraged him in a confrontation. Look how fast he had cooled it when Kester got on the scene.

I had made two mistakes. One was thinking I could really confront anyone. Just because I worked with Kester and Charlie did not mean I was actually "street smart" or could protect myself in the real world of the mean streets of New York.

But my bigger mistake was reverting to some of my old habits of wanting to be in control, to get people to do things I needed them to do. The backpack guy's threat to me had threatened my sense that I was in control, and my ability to do a great job.

Give it up, I told myself. *You are only clean-ing a Starbucks store, not making the world safe for democracy or curing cancer.*

I smiled.

Some of my old friends and family might have thought I *had* contracted cancer by falling so far from the protected and privi-leged life they led, but the unexpected meet-ing with Benjamin that day had reminded me that I had also fallen, like Alice through a rabbit hole, into a great world I could never have imagined . . . where people could be nicer, and the work environment better, than I had ever believed possible.

Or maybe, I thought, as the shuttle pulled into Grand Central, it was more like going through a magic door, like in *The Lion, the Witch and the Wardrobe,* and discovering some sense of wonder and surprise again.

I was tired and felt sleepy, and thought of my little attic apartment with real longing as the last train made its out to Bronxville. I realized I liked the idea of my small apart-ment better than I had ever liked being in the thirty-five-room mansion where I had grown up.

Maybe I was climbing Jacob's ladder, I thought, as I walked up my steep stairs at the end of this long night.

Back off, I told myself. *You are not on some*

high-flying spiritual journey. You are a guy who made a series of stupid mistakes, some like the ones you made tonight, and blew an easy existence. Face it, Mike, I told myself, *you didn't get religion . . . you got broke.*

I admitted at that moment that I would never have found this new world I really loved unless I had had to.

And I had not been on some spiritual journey for the perfect job or satisfying life: I had been caught in a struggle for survival. Which was common for most people in this world, but uncommon for the spoiled prince I had been. Crystal had noticed me, the way you might see someone having trouble swimming, and given me a hand.

What was that famous poem about swimming by Stevie Smith when she says she was not waving but drowning?

My thoughts ran on as I lay in bed.

The scary knife scene was definitely my fault, I decided.

I've got to stop taking myself so seriously, I told myself.

Who, really, was crazier? A sixty-four-year-old man who couldn't give up a sense of power even when it came to cleaning bathrooms, or an angry kid who would be happy to have a confrontation with any old fart who tried to act like an authority figure?

Crystal and my partners at Starbucks, like Kester and Charlie, had given me a chance to work and live and see things a new way. The least I could do was to help them by not reverting to my old, prideful, control-freak self. Yes, I had to admit, I *had* been a control freak, just as much as Ford or any other client. I had loved ordering people to work overtime or change a headline or even bring me a cup of coffee. . . . I had been a real bad boss.

It was time to be a real good Partner.

I promised myself that I would not get so pumped up with ambition or a crazy self-righteous pride in anything I did that I lost my perspective again.

I had a picture of letting my old life go, like you would discard a damp and smelly pair of old swimming trunks.

I had traded my pin-striped suit for a green apron. A Master of the Universe costume for something that said I was there to serve — not to rule.

You can't serve if you try to control the people you serve, I realized.

I wasn't some know-it-all authority, a pompous lifeguard ordering people around on a beach.

I was just another swimmer, now riding a wave I'd never known existed. Starbucks was giving me an incredible ride on a rising tide.

My thoughts tumbled over themselves in a gentle way as I closed my eyes.

"Try a little tenderness," Otis had sung.

I had a picture of myself swimming free-style toward a sunny shore. And then I slept.

7
TURNING LOSERS
INTO WINNERS

"The irony of commitment is that it's deeply liberating — in work, in play, in love. The act frees you from the tyranny of your internal critic, from the fear that likes to dress itself up and parade around as rational hesitation. To commit is to remove your head as the barrier to your life."
— a quote from Anne Morriss, a Starbucks Guest from New York City, published on the side of a Grande Caramel Macchiato

November–December

"Old age is not for sissies," Brooke Astor had famously said.

Several years ago, in my previous life full of major social events, I had met her at many parties. Once, when she was about ninety-seven years old, I could not stop myself from saying how great she looked for her age. (Brooke loves to be complimented for her beauty, which is real, but hates to have it linked to her achievement in growing so old.) "Growing older requires a better and better sense of humor," she told me. I remembered her words, and smiled as I made my way on a cold, gray afternoon into the welcoming warmth of my Starbucks store. *Compared to Brooke, I'm still a kid with a lot of life ahead of me!* I told myself. Yet I had to admit it was absurd to compare myself to the legendary longevity of that society beauty. Mike Gill, working stiff — stiff in almost every muscle after every shift — was no Brooke Astor!

Crystal greeted me as soon as I stepped inside the store.

"Mike, I've got a new idea for you."

There were many Guests milling around, and Crystal led me over to a corner in the front of the store, by the bean wall.

"Look." She gestured. "See all those pounds of coffee beans?"

I nodded slowly. The last several months of fall — as the weather cooled off and my spirits picked up — I had been getting more and more confident in what I had been doing in cleaning, opening, and closing at the store. So I greeted Crystal's new idea for what I could do with a little trepidation, and also without much enthusiasm.

In my previous life, when I was younger and was confident of earning a good living, I had loved new challenges.

"You're going to London to present the idea one-on-one with the client," Don Robertson, a boss of mine, once said. "And don't come back unless you sell our campaign to Marks and Spencer." My heart had once leapt at that kind of challenge. With the arrogance of youth, I didn't think I could fail. Partly because of my naïve confidence, I was usually successful. Now, with the insecurity of advancing age and many personal and professional failures, I hesitated before *any* new challenges.

Crystal and Starbucks had been my life raft in a tumultuous time, but I was already too far outside my comfort zone at the store to try new things successfully.

And my job at Starbucks was too important to me to risk losing by trying something new. I had been out of work too long to take on any new challenges, even if they were from Crystal.

Crystal saw the concern in my face.

"Don't worry, Mike," she said. "This is right for you. Don't you like coffee?"

"I love coffee."

"Wasn't that how I met you . . . coming in for a Latte?"

"Y . . . e . . . s . . . ," I said, more slowly.

"This is your chance to share your love with others. Remember how I gave you a sample of coffee and pastries on your first day?"

"I'll never forget it." I smiled happily at the memory. "It really got me excited about working here with you."

"I know. But believe it or not, Mike, many Partners don't like coffee that much."

I looked around at the Partners. Lovely, little Bianca was working the register. Tall, elegant Anthony was at the espresso bar. They were both about nineteen, and they never made themselves coffee drinks. I knew what Crystal said was true. At the beginning of each shift, every Partner was allowed free libations. The other Partners were all young, and most of them liked Frappuccinos and sweet drinks, like a lot of other young people. They rarely ordered real coffee straight, not even Lattes and Cappuccinos. In contrast to the other Partners, I was always making myself a coffee. Coffee was a real treat for me. One of the great perks of working at Starbucks.

Crystal was right.

Maybe there was a way to share my love of coffee with others. But how?

As though reading my mind, Crystal said:

"At Starbucks we have Coffee Masters."

Crystal paused, as though giving me time to contemplate a big idea, but the very word "master" had set off a memory of when my father had introduced me to Frank Lloyd Wright and he had told me that people who worked with the great architect called him "the Master." I had felt back then the awe and admiration my father had for that title. Now I was to become a "Master" — a "*Coffee* Master." The thought made me smile.

But Crystal was serious about what she was saying. She didn't smile back. "It's not easy to become a Coffee Master, Mike. You have to master a knowledge of a lot of coffees, and then one of your jobs is to sample the coffee with Partners and Guests —"

"I would love that," I interrupted her.

"Exactly!" She laughed. "Mike, you are funny. Don't you get it? That's why I thought of *you* to have this role. See all these beans?"

Crystal gestured at the packages of coffee behind us. She was dressed in a white silk shirt that gleamed with a special brightness against her green apron. Her hair was pulled back, highlighting her face. When I was casting for beautiful women in television commercials, I had been told by some research person: "Look for high cheekbones . . . a

239

symmetrical balance of features in the face. From the Greeks to Jessica Simpson, that has been the criterion for beauty for thousands of years." Crystal had that beauty.

"There's no point in having all those beans on display unless people know about the coffee."

It was suddenly clear to me: Starbucks was about coffee, and the more that people could understand and appreciate the coffee, the better off we would all be.

"You get a black apron," Crystal said, "and I can just see you on the floor greeting the Guests, inviting them to sample the coffee while you tell them all about it."

"Feels good to me," I said.

" 'Feels good' is the right response," Crystal said, pointing toward my heart. "Follow your *heart.* That's what I tell all my Partners. And your heart is clearly in the coffee."

It did feel good. I did feel confident. I felt this was something I could do, and enjoy doing.

"Plus," Crystal added, "you're great with our Guests."

Under Crystal's guidance I took a series of computer courses. It was almost like going to coffee college. There were different subject areas: the history, geography, growing conditions, and every aspect of great coffee making. I found out where coffee was first discovered, how it was grown, and harvested, and dried or washed, and shipped, and then roasted. The roasting, it turned out, was as important as the selection and the growing in determining the final taste. I discovered that Starbucks was extremely picky about their kinds of coffee, helping farmers grow the best crops in the best conditions for the community and the environment. Of course, Starbucks only bought a tiny percentage of the world's coffee and could afford to make sure they got the best. I came to understand how Starbucks had a patented way to keep coffee fresh when they shipped the beans to the stores, and why freshness was one of the key elements in making great coffee.

I also filled out my "Coffee Passport," a small book with room for taste reactions to many varieties, putting the labels in as I sampled coffee, giving an opinion as to the flavor, body, acidity, and all the aspects of aroma and "mouth feel" of the various blends and single-origin brews.

After a couple of weeks of hard studies, Crystal told me, "The holidays are coming up. Why don't you plan some coffee seminars and samplings for our Partners and

Guests?"

In the coming days, Crystal helped me make up signs.

For my first seminar I chose Yukon because it was a coffee with a great story.

I picked a date, an evening in early December. With Crystal's help I put up a sign, inviting people to sample coffee, along with free oatmeal raisin cookies and chocolate chunk cookies. Raisins and oatmeal go well with Yukon, and chocolate is a kissing cousin of all coffees. Chocolate and coffee always make for a great taste combination. They were also my favorite cookies. My new role as Coffee Master allowed me to plan my own events featuring the food and coffee I thought would be best.

As I worked nervously, with some anxiety, to set up the pastries for the upcoming Coffee Tasting, for some reason a picture of my having blundered in a tea with the queen of England came into my mind. It was a semiformal event in a tent during a polo match many years ago. I had inadvertently upset Queen Elizabeth's arm when I rushed to reach for a cucumber sandwich on a table beside her. I had developed a passion for those elegant combinations of cucumbers sliced wafer thin and gently placed between soft pieces of white bread. I had moved too quickly in my anxiety to grab a sandwich, and I'd upset the delicate social balance of that occasion. The queen gave me a bit of a frown, but her husband, the duke of Edinburgh, just a step behind, dressed for polo, was clearly displeased and physically brushed me back as though I were some kind of intruding barbarian. I did not get my sandwich, and it had been a humiliating social experience for me at what should have been a relaxed occasion.

Why had that awkward, embarrassing moment come into my mind now? Because I was working so hard to make sure everyone enjoyed the coffee and pastries I would serve, and hoped nothing would go wrong? Because I felt like a host who must not make some unintentional mistake that could cause frowns instead of smiles?

I told myself that the coffee and cookies would be a hit, and Crystal had said that several Guests had checked with her, after seeing our invitations, to make sure of the time. So I reminded myself to be confident. How upset could people be after being served cookies and coffee? I ground up some fresh Yukon for a French press, filled it with hot water, timed it four minutes, and then served it in little sample cups, along with the cookies. There were a dozen Guests who had come to hear about the coffee and get the free treats.

Rachel's husband, Justin, was there. He often accompanied his wife and his child, Max, to Starbucks, but they were not with him tonight.

"Where's Rachel and Max?"

"Home. Rachel is still staying on Decaf. This is an hour out for me!" He laughed.

Dr. Paul had come, without his Red Sox hat.

"Where's the hat?"

"The Sox don't need me anymore. Now I'm guilty for having given them the World Series. You can't win!"

There was a petite, white-haired woman who came in each day for a Venti . . . our largest, twenty-ounce coffee. She was obviously a passionate coffee lover.

There was also a young couple, clearly in love. They kept holding hands and laughing into each other's eyes. I thought at first they were there by accident, so I asked them, "Do you want to be part of this coffee tasting?"

"That's why we came," the young man said. "We met each other here over coffee," he said.

"And we like coffee," she said, and they laughed as though she had made a wonderful joke.

I liked their laughter. I remembered that Crystal had told me that the original vision of Starbucks had been based on an Italian café. I imagined there would be a lot of laughter in that kind of place.

I had a little silver tray, and each guest picked up a small cup and a cookie.

"We are sampling Yukon coffee this evening," I announced to the audience. "First, smell," I said. "Then slurp, *then* speak."

They laughed again — the young couple and the whole little group. I laughed too, an unforced laugh that just came out naturally. I was happy standing there leading this seminar in a subject I had grown to love.

"While you enjoy," I said, "here's a little history. There is no coffee grown in the Yukon . . . so why the name?"

The small group looked up happily. . . . The wonderful coffee and cookies were already doing their work. In addition, they all seemed to be genuinely interested.

Crystal and Kester approached, and I served them samples of coffee and pastries. Kester gave me a wink and a big smile. I knew he wasn't really into coffee; he was just there for moral support.

Crystal was a stickler for anything related

to serving coffee. She sipped her coffee seriously. Then she smiled. I breathed a sigh of relief. I had prepared Yukon right.

"The reason it's called Yukon," I continued, "is because a fishing boat captain in Seattle who made trips to the Yukon came in and said he needed a stronger brew than the popular House Blend. So they blended in some bolder Indonesian coffee along with the Latin American beans."

"It's good," Dr. Paul said.

"Delicious," Rachel's husband said.

The white-haired lady nodded her head enthusiastically.

Several other Guests also murmured their appreciation. We got into a further discussion of coffees, how volcanic soil in Indonesia made for particularly delicious beans. I mentioned Sumatra, my first love, and also Sulawesi, another Indonesian coffee that was a little more subtle, more elegant. I promised we would sample them next time.

I noticed that Crystal and Kester had drifted away, back to their Starbucks duties. I took that as a vote of confidence. I knew that Crystal would not have let me continue the seminar if she felt I was doing anything wrong. She trusted me.

"Who discovered coffee?" I turned to greet the question asked by a man I called

246

the Professor. He taught a course at Columbia. He had a white beard and sparkling green eyes. He always had a Solo Espresso "for here," he'd say. Which meant he wanted it served in a porcelain cup. He'd stay in our store to savor his espresso shot, reading his book while he sipped his expresso.

"Good question, Professor," I said. "Coffee first originated in Ethiopia. We have a great coffee called Ethiopia Sidamo. There is a wonderful story about the beginning of coffee, although it might be a bit metaphorical . . . more of an allegory."

"I like mystic myths," the Professor said with a smile.

"One day," I began, "hundreds of years ago, a goat herder followed his goats up the hills of Ethiopia. He was a young boy, and the goats led him farther and farther up the slopes. The goats moved so fast, at one point they left the boy behind. He was a poet, and had a flute, and he probably paused to create a song. When he caught up with the goats, they were chewing berries and dancing on their hind legs. The young boy was entranced by that exciting sight. The boy started chewing the berries, and soon he was dancing too." I continued, "When he came home, dancing and singing, his family also wanted to know what was going on . . .

so they went up the hill to get some of these magic berries. Over the course of centuries the Ethiopians learned to roast the beans . . . and other people took the coffee plants from Ethiopia. A Frenchman brought a plant to Latin America in the eighteenth century, and the Dutch brought some to Indonesia even earlier."

"I love that story," said the Professor. "I can't wait to have some Ethiopian coffee."

"How about we do a sampling next week?" I hadn't checked with Crystal, but why not?

"Great," Dr. Paul said.

"It's a date," the young couple said, and laughed again.

Gradually the group broke up, some staying to ask more specific questions about coffee beans. Several of the Guests bought pound bags of Yukon to take home.

As I cleaned up, I heard Frank Sinatra on the Starbucks speakers.

"That's life," Frank sang. I remembered meeting him one night in Toots Shor's bar in New York. The bar was a favorite for some of us who had just left college and started to work in the big city. The mood was always festive in the barnlike bar, but the big appeal was Toots himself. He was the ideal bar host. He was drinking right along with you. And he had one more great quality we young guys really needed: He would cash our checks. This was long before ATMs; even credit cards were uncommon. Often, we needed some cash late at night. No problem with Toots. It was a feeling of power to be given cash with a simple check: We could then all buy another round.

Frank had come in late one night when I was drinking with some friends. Sometimes, when you have seen someone's face so often on TV or in the movies, you feel you know them. I had grown up with Frank Sinatra, and as he entered the bar, I instinctively called out as if to a friend, "Hi, Frank!"

When I realized that he wasn't a friend but *Frank Sinatra* himself, I was embarrassed, but he was kind to us and paused to say hello. He soon made his way to the back to get insulted by Toots — who was famous for calling everyone "ya bum, ya" — but he had paused just long enough to make us feel good.

I loved to hear him sing. Now, as I started to sing along, I saw Anthony looking over at me. Anthony was just nineteen, but seemed much older. He always arrived with highly polished brown shoes and pants that had clearly been freshly pressed. Above all, Anthony always had a kind, confident smile on his face — even when facing a long line, he never lost his classy cool.

"Frank Sinatra's a great singer," I told him, still full of upbeat energy from the coffee seminar and the music.

Anthony gave me a quizzical look. He had clearly never heard of the man who had been such an icon. This was often the case with the music played at Starbucks. The young Partners didn't pick the music we played. It was chosen by people in Seattle who seemed to love the old recording artists that I had grown up with. Our Guests also seemed to relate to the old singers: They had made the CDs by Ray Charles and Frank Sinatra bestsellers at our store.

"Frank was like you," I told Anthony, trying to get him to understand on some level what the singer had meant to those of my generation. "He was a real stylish gentleman. People said he could be rude, but I met him once and he went out of his way to be nice to me . . . when I was just about your age."

"Sounds good," said Anthony, and then he laughed, catching himself in a kind of pun about the sounds of the singer that were now surrounding us as we talked. I could see he was being kind to me and was really not much interested in the idea of Frank Sinatra. I suddenly realized that

Frank had *died* before Anthony was *born.*

"He's ancient history to you," I said.

"*You* are a history lesson," Anthony said.

He could see the stricken look on my face. I hated to be reminded that I was decades older than the Partners.

"But I *like* history," Anthony said, eager to make me feel better.

"Me too," I said, talking fast in my embarrassment and also hoping to make something positive out of this. "I studied history at school."

"Me too," Anthony said, also wanting to make sure in his gentlemanly way that we could relate at some level. "I plan to go to college and take some history. Starbucks pays for courses," he told me, as though confiding some special secret, "and I plan to take all I can."

Anthony was being kind to me, but I was grateful for his courteous style. And I was sure Anthony was the kind of disciplined guy who would graduate. I wasn't so sure about Yvette. She would show up with books, but she also was always complaining about not having enough time to study. My heart went out to her: I could imagine what it was like to try to go to school and work the shifts at Starbucks. Starbucks helping out with education, even for part-time employees, was great, but it still took a Partner with a lot of heart and discipline to make use of the opportunity. Anthony didn't seem to be struggling to balance work and school. I was sure he was going to use Starbucks to help him achieve *his* goals.

I was smiling, thinking about Anthony and his classy style and positive ambition, as I made my way back behind the bar.

Crystal was still in her little office space. She looked up.

"One happy guy," she said, noticing my upbeat mood. "Mike, you *are* funny."

"What do you mean?"

I was still a little defensive about — and confused by — her way of describing me.

"I don't know," she said, moving around to face me. "Like you had that whole group laughing at the coffee seminar."

"It is a pretty funny story about the goat herder. . . ."

"It's not just the story, Mike. Guests like it that you're happy here."

"Yeah," I said. I moved past her to go downstairs, where I took off my apron and threw it in the laundry pile. I didn't want to think about how happy I was. I was almost superstitious about it. I wasn't used to feeling like this.

Back upstairs, I clocked out and headed

for the door.

"Great job," Crystal called after me. "We'll do a lot more of these. . . . The holidays will be good for us!"

The next seminar and sampling I scheduled was a comparison between Sulawesi and Sumatra. Sumatra had a heavier mouth feel and a more definitive, "earthy" taste, while Sulawesi had a more elegant, complicated set of flavors to be enjoyed.

Growing in confidence with the Starbucks experience, I asked Annie to come on the night of the tasting. I was happy to see her in the crowd. She brought her boyfriend.

It was another great tasting. This time, a group of about twenty people of all ages had gathered. They really got into describing the differences. I served some espresso brownies with the Sulawesi and some espresso beans coated with peanut butter for the Sumatra — both big taste treats.

Annie and her boyfriend hung back shyly during the tasting, but afterward she came up to me.

"A new star on Broadway," she said, giving me a big hug and kiss. Annie herself loved the theater and performing. I saw what she meant. Starbucks was a kind of theater. A theater of good times. A unique place people could come that wasn't work and wasn't home. They could relax and get away from all the details that filled their minds, and just feel good for a change.

Partners *were* kind of performing, greeting people with an upbeat mood that lifted their lives. And, of course, serving coffee and pastries that also made them feel better.

Some say we have gone from the Industrial Age to a Consumer Society to an Entertainment Age. Starbucks Partners were certainly interested in entertainers.

I mentioned to Charlie one night that my daughter Bis was making a film in Ireland with 50 Cent. I had never heard of him, but Bis told me: "Your Partners will know who he is."

Charlie sure did. Always high energy, he almost became airborne when he heard the name.

"50 Cent!" he yelled. "Hey, Kester, Mike knows 50 Cent!"

"No, no," I hastened to interrupt. "I don't know him!" In fact, it was true. I had never even heard any songs by him. I didn't even know what he *looked* like. Bis had told me he was "really very sweet," but I doubted that secondhand knowledge would go over well.

Kester came over. Bianca joined the group

gathering around me. Even though there was a line of guests waiting to be served, they couldn't resist hearing more about 50 Cent.

"What's he like?" Bianca asked. "Is he really bad?"

"He's supposed to be a nice guy, my daughter says. . . ."

"Let's get back to the line," Kester said, reminding us all to focus on serving the Guests. Later, at the end of my shift, Charlie came up to me.

"So tell me about 50 Cent."

"My daughter knows him," I said. "I never met him. . . . It's just that my *daughter* is making a film with him."

Charlie didn't seem to be put off by the fact that I was far from a fan or a friend of 50 Cent. I caught the excitement even *any* connection to such a popular entertainer had for my Partners. I think Charlie, and maybe, in their heart of hearts, *all* of them, could, in some way at some time, see themselves making that move from a Starbucks Partner to famous entertainer. 50 Cent had made the move, and it was not impossible for them.

I could catch their enthusiasm for the entertainment world. So being on Broadway "performing" by creating a great experience for our Guests was not far from the natural inclination and ambition of the Partners. In that sense, Starbucks was also very much in the Entertainment Age, with drinks and music and a warm welcome by Partners who threw themselves into their roles.

I felt better and better about my role in the store: serving coffee I loved to people I really enjoyed talking with.

I went back to clean up.

Crystal was going over some business reports.

She seemed in a great mood. I realized she was happy for me. That was a nice feeling.

"Mike, take a look at this. . . ." She pointed to her computer screen.

"Our bean sales are way up . . . and studies show the more beans you sell, the more loyal Guests you get."

"Good," I said, staring dumbly at the screen, not really understanding all the numbers I was seeing. I knew there was a whole dimension of Starbucks that was foreign to me. Somewhere, somehow, they calibrated every sale. I had little interest in figures and data.

Crystal turned to look at me. The blank look on my face must have revealed my inability to comprehend the numbers on the screen, but she wanted me to appreciate something.

"You're helping the store, Mike."

She paused.

"You're helping me."

I was so grateful to Crystal for saving me from my downward spiral, and to be able to help her in some small way was a great feeling.

"There's an Open Forum . . . a chance for all the Partners in *this* region to get together, next week. Kester's coming, Yvette and Anthony. *All* the Partners in our store and in this region are invited. I'd like you to come with us."

The next week I went to the Forum. It was held in the bottom of an old cathedral on the Lower East Side. Hundreds of Partners were there. Some, like myself, wore the typical Starbucks clothes — black or tan pants, black or white shirts — but others had street clothes on. At the door we were all given new Starbucks T-shirts celebrating the season. As I entered the room, I saw that there were tables filled with such popular drinks as Pumpkin Spice Latte and Peppermint Mocha — all, of course, free for us.

I was stopped as I entered by a man who said his name was Tom from Personnel. He asked me how things were going, and if he could do anything more for me. I told him things were great and asked him if *I* could do anything more for Starbucks. "Just find more people with a positive attitude like yours," he told me. That made me feel good.

I looked around for Crystal and saw her talking with Kester up at the front of the room. Someone grabbed my arm. It was Yvette. Yvette was almost as tall as me, and now she had her hair all piled up on top of her head. There was a rule in the store that you always had to wear a Starbucks hat, so most Partners kept their hair tight so it could fit underneath. This was a whole new Yvette. She was also wearing a very non-Starbucks type of gold tank top and a small red skirt. I also noticed she had a tattoo of a heart on her arm. I had never seen that before because it was a dress code rule at Starbucks that you had to cover *any* tattoos when you were on the floor serving Guests.

Yvette seemed like a changed woman.

"Let's go sample some of those drinks."

We walked over to a long table where they were setting up little samples.

"Would you like to sample our Egg Nog Latte?" a young lady asked.

"Sure," we said.

It was delicious, at least to me. Yvette was

less impressed.

"Any Frappuccinos?" Yvette asked.

"We've got a new Double Chocolate Chip Frappuccino. Would you like a sample?" We each had a little cup of the iced drink. As we sipped, the lady said: "Frappuccinos were invented in California, by Partners in a store in Santa Monica. Their Guests asked for smoothies, which were popular out there. But our Partners thought of a way to mix coffee and ice that was —"

"Nice," Yvette interrupted, giggling like a young kid at her own joke. Beneath her almost shocking getup — at least to me — she was still the struggling student I knew.

"Right," the young woman behind the counter said, smiling. "So remember, we are *always* happy to take suggestions about Partner ideas."

"Cool," Yvette said, taking my arm again, smiling back at the lady, and moving us on.

"Look at that!" she said, pointing across the room.

Yvette had seen a booth with a bunch of cute Christmas teddy bears. Starbucks created little bears for every season. They were very popular with the Partners and with the Guests.

Crystal came over as we reached the booth. She picked up a bear.

"These are beautifully made," Crystal said. "I've got a whole collection back at my apartment."

I was not surprised. Crystal's passion for Starbucks was an integral part of her life. Why wouldn't she want to be surrounded by Starbucks bears at work *and* at home?

"You can win a bear," a young man told us from behind the counter of the booth, "if you answer some questions about Starbucks. But the questions aren't easy."

"Let's win," Crystal said, typically confident.

"Who is going to play?" the young man asked.

"We will all play . . . a Partner *team* from Broadway!"

"Good," the man said. "This is a kind of Starbucks trivia game. You have to know a lot of facts to win."

"Let's go," Yvette said. Yvette was always in a hurry. My image of her was a young woman running in just to be on time for the beginning of her shift, and then running out again at the end of work to make her next vital appointment.

"Here's a question," the man said. "What was the original color of the Starbucks logo?"

"Brown," Crystal answered in a heartbeat.

"Wow!" I said.

"I know all this stuff," Crystal said.

"Where does the name Starbucks come from?"

There was an uneasy silence. Crystal clearly didn't know this answer, and I was sure Yvette had no idea. So it was up to me. Fortunately, as soon as I had joined Starbucks, I had started to read all about it. I loved history, and Starbucks had an unusual one.

"Starbuck was the first mate on a ship," I said.

"A ship?" the man said. He was not going to let us win a bear so easily.

"Captain Ahab's boat . . . searching for Moby-Dick. Starbuck liked coffee, or something like that."

I had once read somewhere that while they had chosen the name, the young men who founded Starbucks were not quite clear about the actual story. Like most of us in that generation, they had been supposed to "read" *Moby-Dick* but had actually glanced through it rapidly. *Moby-Dick,* like Joyce's *Ulysses,* was a book everyone at school was required to read, but most never really did.

"Anything else about the name?" the young man asked.

"The name is great," I said, feeling good

now that I had answered his first question correctly.

I could tell Crystal was pleased with me, and Yvette had given my arm a squeeze.

"Starbucks is a name," I said, "that is *unique,* easy to *pronounce,* and implies key *benefits.*"

These were proven rules for names I had written down when I was a creative director, for my clients who were interested in inventing new names. "The Trifecta of the Great Name Game" I had called these crucial criteria.

The young man in the booth was staring at me. . . . *Where did this crazy guy come from?* he probably wondered.

Crystal was smiling; she knew me by now and how I could go off into advertising speak when given half a chance. Yvette was bored and looking around for the next place to be.

"I just meant," I said quickly, "everyone wants to be a *star,* and everyone wants to make *bucks.* So Star . . . bucks is a perfect name."

The man behind the counter laughed loud, and so did Crystal and Yvette. Even a couple of people who were just standing around joined in heartfelt laughter after hearing my explanation of why the Starbucks name had such a powerful appeal.

I had struck a chord with my comment. And obviously no Partner had thought of that happy conjunction before.

"You win a bear," the man said, handing over to me a little bear dressed up as Santa Claus.

I handed the bear to Crystal.

She took it carefully.

"Look at this," she said. "Velvet. Hand-stitched. This is going home!"

Yvette was heading off to another part of the room. Maybe she had seen someone she wanted to talk to, or something more exciting going on.

Crystal and I started to walk away.

"That's a good one about the name. *Star . . . bucks.* I'll remember that," the young man called.

Crystal and I walked up and took some seats near the front. Gradually the seats behind us filled up as Crystal carefully put the bear into her commodious, luxurious leather bag.

"You really are a funny guy, Mike," Crystal said. "Knowing all that stuff."

"About the name?" I asked.

"I don't just mean funny in the sense of funny. Although you do make me laugh." Crystal smiled. "I just mean the way you enjoy the Guests, and talking with the Partners. You seemed so cold and serious when I first met you. You have really lightened up. I guess that's what I mean by funny. Now you really enjoy Starbucks. I can tell."

She gave me a kind look.

"I think we are alike that way. You get it, Mike. But it's just kind of weird," she laughed. "I just never expected . . . you know, we'd have some laughs. And I never thought you'd get me a *bear!*"

Kester sat down next to me, and Anthony also joined us.

"Mike won me a bear," Crystal said, gesturing toward her bag.

I hadn't realized that all my hard work in cleaning and the coffee seminars and everything would be less important than this small achievement. But maybe the bear was just a symbol to Crystal of my being close to her wavelength. I didn't want to analyze it to death. It felt good.

"Cool" was all Kester said, but he gave me a gentle punch on my shoulder. I felt I was in sync with my Partners.

Soon a woman took the stage. She was in her late thirties. She stood tall and straight and was clearly confident in speaking before such a large audience.

"Hi," she said, "I'm Kathy. I hope you are all having a good time today."

There was a small cheer from the audience.

"They call me a regional director, but really I'm just a person you can go to when you want some answers. So let's get going! We are here to answer *any* Partners' questions. . . ."

"How do I get a music CD I made with some friends sold in the stores?" a Partner asked. There were other questions along those lines.

"Great question," Kathy would say, and then mention a name the questioner should call. Often that person was there. There was someone who represented the music department, and the pastries, and cleaning the stores — all the different aspects of our lives. So the questions could be answered in real time. I was impressed. We had never held an Open Forum at JWT where all the employees could ask any question. It had never occurred to us. *If we're happy, our employees should be happy* was really the philosophy of the top management.

After the questions had continued for about an hour, Kathy said, "And now for the entertainment."

Kathy and a bunch of people from management came out onstage dressed as rock stars and danced to a new CD Starbucks was then selling. The Partners in the audience loved it. That top management could make fools of themselves in such a public forum showed that no Partner had to be afraid. It was more proof to me that Starbucks *was* in the entertainment business.

After the "show," Kathy announced, "Now we have a few awards to give out. Let's start with the top award: Best Manager of the Year . . . Moses Thornton!"

A big cheer went up as a young African-American man made his way to the stage.

Kathy read out an award praising all his qualities and the performance of his store. More applause.

"Our next award," Kathy said, "goes to someone who has done a great job for many years . . . and it is my pleasure to present the Manager of the Quarter Award to Crystal Thompson."

Crystal gave a little gasp and leapt up. The whole room seemed to come to their feet. She was clearly a popular choice. As she made her way to the stage, everyone started clapping.

Crystal waved to me and Kester, and to all her other friends in the crowd.

I realized again I was by far the oldest

person in the room. These young people had a kind of energy and enthusiasm I imagined you might find at a rock concert — although I had never attended one myself.

How different this was from my experience in advertising. Anytime I had won an award there, I could immediately sense the competitive anger in the room, barely disguised by polite hand clapping.

Here, it was clear everyone was happy for Crystal. They knew how hard she worked. They liked her. And I think they also knew that they had a good chance to be recognized themselves in the future. The advertising world was based on a pyramid where only a few got to enjoy the recognition. At Starbucks *everyone* was respected, and many, if not most, were recognized . . . not just at special forums, but every day, in every store.

The Forum was just another example to me of what a wonderful group I was now part of. I was thrilled for Crystal — she was the *true* star on Broadway.

As we moved into the holiday season, I found that doing successful Coffee Tastings and the general increased activity of my store were a help to me in my lonely and disoriented state. In my previous life, at this time of year, when I was still living with my wife and children in a small Connecticut mountain town, my holiday world would have been full with the constant comings and goings of family and friends. My old New England farmhouse — like a Currier and Ives print come to life — would have been full of the sounds and sights and smells of Christmas.

Living alone in my small apartment by the train tracks in the suburbs was very different. The loudest sound in my apartment was the abrupt honk of the trains as they drove through the station just hundreds of feet away. What had happened, I wondered, to the romantic whistles of the old steam engines that Thomas Wolfe had found so full of the promise of new adventures as they echoed in the Smoky Mountains around his beloved Asheville home? The abrupt train honks that shattered my silence sounded like the inhuman bleatings of robotic beings. The title of one of Wolfe's books echoed in my mind: *You Can't Go Home Again.* That was certainly true for me during these holidays. My former home was now off-limits.

So I was grateful to leave the confinement of my empty apartment and join in the animated spirit and human interaction of the holidays at my Starbucks store. Behind the register, and out in front doing my Coffee Tastings and pastry samplings, I was part of a convivial group, and the constant pain and guilt I felt deep in my heart at all the hurt I had caused — more intense during these "family holidays" — was partially subdued or — from time to time — forgotten entirely in the rush of activity working the frantic shifts in my store. The store was crowded, there was more work to do, and I had now learned how to do it better, and got some pride in helping my Partners — rather than always being the one who needed help.

I would try to see my son Jonathan at least once or twice a week. I had bought him some little wooden trains, and we would play with these — moving them up and down the floor. It was a relief to be with him. He had no painful questions for me and a great talent to find positive wonder in each moment. As I nurtured him, he nurtured me. It was a peaceful, renewing zone to be with Jonathan and to watch his delight as he moved the trains back and forth. We would make up adventures for them within a few feet of floor space. Sometimes a little blue engine might need help. He would glide a coal car from one spot to another.

Another time he might leap up with a graceful, fluid motion, to move a chair or some other obstacle blocking the way of our train. I could share Jonathan's uninhibited enjoyment of the moment and leave my sense of loss and my fear of the future far behind.

My daughter Bis was in Ireland working on her movie, but my other children were home for the holidays — in Connecticut, where I was no longer welcome. I called them, and we talked, but it was often awkward and painful despite their efforts and my attempt to keep things as positive as possible. The one part of my present life they seemed to respect was that they knew I was struggling hard to make it in a job that was not easy for me and did not build on my former need for status.

And my job had become much more than simply "a job" during the holiday season, as Crystal and my Partners filled up the void in my life with a kind of cheerful, purposeful energy that was a relief to me. I was not invited to holiday parties in the houses of my previous friends, and I would not have felt comfortable going if I had been. I did not want to cause more pain to the family and friends I had already hurt, by showing up like a ghost of Christmas past.

My Starbucks store became a refuge for

me in a turbulent, emotional time. My store on old Broadway was a little like an island of warm welcome in the larger island of Manhattan, where I was learning to survive and to make new connections. In a very real sense it had become my new home for the holidays. I realized now how much affection I felt for Crystal and my Partners. And I felt real admiration for the great job they were doing, and helping *me* to do. I liked the growing confidence I felt in being able to contribute in some small but practical ways to my store's success. That I — an old guy literally on his "last legs" — could still add some value to my Partners' lives also helped to give me a feeling I could still add some worth to the world.

Going out the door of my store after another successful Coffee Tasting, I was met with a gust of cold December air. The weather had changed dramatically in the last few days. I pulled down my wool hat and pulled on my wool gloves.

As I walked toward the subway, the lights seemed brighter in the city. Maybe it was a trick of the dropping temperature. They seemed to twinkle magically in the arctic air.

I started walking, then literally stopped with a shock of revelation: "I am happier than I have ever been," I said out loud.

Fortunately, in New York City, many people speak loudly to themselves, and nobody notices.

I took off a glove I had just put on.

I put my hand on my heart.

I could feel a kind of gentle, inner happiness I had never felt before.

What was going on?

I was almost scared; still afraid to admit to myself how happy I was now . . . with a job as a barista at Starbucks. This was not the high-status job or affluent life my parents, my family, and my friends had expected of me.

Did this mean that my whole former life — all sixty-four years of it — had been a joke?

No. I shook my head, still planted in the spot, arguing with myself. I had loved many things. I *still* loved my children. But I had to admit, for the first time and with a brutal honesty, that I had hated large swatches of my former, high-status life, full of so much meaningless activity.

I took a turn around the corner, and back up Broadway. I wanted to walk for a while. I had to think. I didn't want to go underground too fast tonight. The lights were too bright.

What was I thinking?

I hated to think that my whole life had been a lie.

But I had to admit that I felt great relief in the different life I had now . . . even my little apartment. I felt proud of being able to live and support myself. . . . Still . . . it did not make sense. I had achieved at sixty-four what most people accomplish by twenty-four. Why was I so happy?

I felt my heart again.

The gentle love and peace and happiness I felt now I had never experienced before.

Maybe the mistakes I had made — causing so much damage — had also helped me to break out of my comfortable cocoon . . . to get out to a world so much more full of life and light.

I didn't know. I couldn't really *think* it through.

But I knew what I felt in my heart.

Crystal had said: "Follow your heart."

My heart was full of a happiness I had never known before.

I should have known that things were bound to change.

8
FIRED — ALMOST

"Every day is a leap of faith."
— a quote from Lizz Wright, musician,
published on the side of a cup of a
Short Americano

January

As I entered into the warmth of the store one cold January morning, Tawana greeted me with a baleful stare that canceled the goodwill I was feeling.

"Crystal wants to see you," Tawana told me, with a look of cold satisfaction that stopped my heart.

Those were not good words, especially from Tawana. While other Partners always made an effort, no matter how busy they were, to greet me with a smile and a verbal welcome, Tawana was frosty. Working with adversaries made a good job unpleasant. I couldn't help but remember another scene from my past, sitting in the grand Algonquin Hotel on Forty-fourth Street with my father when I was sixteen.

"I despise that man," my father said, gesturing with his hand toward a large, elderly man sitting in a chair across the room, who seemed to be staring back across the lobby of the Algonquin Hotel through a thick pair of glasses.

My father reached for the peanuts in the bowl in the center of the table. He threw a fistful into his mouth. My father had been a fat teenager and was always fearful of gaining weight, but he could not resist peanuts. In fact, he seemed to survive almost solely on peanuts from the Algonquin or served at cocktail parties, and would almost never sit down to eat a regular meal. He certainly was never at home for dinner. This evening my father seemed to be munching his peanuts with a special intensity.

"That is James Thurber," my father said. "I hate him, and I think the feeling is mutual."

I had heard of James Thurber. He was a man whose words and pictures were original, and were regularly published in *The New Yorker*. I had actually studied one of his humorous short stories at school and told my father about it just the day before.

"Recently I told others at the office about a scandalous, funny story Truman Capote had told me about Thurber," my father continued, "and aroused Thurber's undying ire. Thurber doesn't really have a sense of humor about himself."

I was also familiar with Truman Capote, although I had not yet read any book by him.

"Truman was the most beautiful creature any of us had ever seen when he first appeared at the magazine." My father smiled, lighting up his face and the mood as he launched fully into his storytelling manner. He eyes sparkled, and he sat up straighter in the chair. He could have been addressing a small audience of adoring fans. I was relieved. My father telling a story was at his best.

"Thurber treated Truman like an office boy, asking him to do the most degrading things. Thurber is virtually blind. He would have assignations with women in the afternoon, right here in this hotel, and then call Truman over to help him get dressed. One day, Truman, in dressing him, reversed his socks so Thurber's wife would know that he had been undressed during the day."

I smiled. It sounded funny, and I, as a young boy with no such problems, could easily picture the discomfiture of the old man when his wife, undressing him that night, had discovered his adultery.

I could also understand how my father would think that the story was relatively harmless to pass on. My father loved gossip, especially sexual gossip, especially about famous people, and told such stories with fervor and almost a pride of purpose that bordered on the manic.

But I was also surprised that Thurber or anyone at his beloved magazine could hate my father. He seemed so eager early every morning to leave the house for his office, and to come home so late, I imagined his *New Yorker* colleagues as having one happy time, almost a constant positive party atmosphere. So Thurber's negative emotion was a new idea for me.

I thought of Thurber's and my father's ill will as I walked back to Crystal's little office. While my relationship with Tawana was worlds apart from that of my father and Thurber's, I realized that negativity anywhere, from anyone, could drag you down in many ways. I was afraid that Tawana was trying to sabotage the one good thing to happen to me in a long time.

I told myself to calm down. I was doing the best I could, that would have to be enough, whatever happened. I remembered the times when I had given that exact advice to my kids when they were under pressure: When Bis was having trouble with a sadistic teacher in high school, when my son Charles was involved in a crazy lacrosse tournament, I had assured them that all would be well if they just focused on doing the best they could. Now I realized that giving such commonsense advice was easy, but taking it was hard. Despite my attempts to stay calm, my heart was beating with some anxiety as I headed back to talk with Crystal.

As I entered the office, Crystal looked up, but did not smile.

Bianca was with her. "Will you give us a minute?" Crystal asked Bianca, who gave me one of her sweet little smiles, turned, and left us alone.

Another bad sign. What was Crystal going to say to me that she could not share with another Partner?

"Sit down, Mike," Crystal said, still not smiling. A final, bad sign. There was one other little chair in the cramped space, but most discussions took place without anyone sitting down . . . unless they were on a meal break.

"Tawana has brought something to my attention. . . ."

Crystal paused, clearly searching for the right way to say something serious to me.

"She has pointed out that you have been more than ten dollars over and, once, more than ten dollars short at different times during the last month."

Crystal was referring to the cash register count we did at the end of every shift. I knew you were supposed to be within five dollars over and under — at the most.

I hastened to interrupt. "I'm sorry."

"Sorry is good," Crystal said, "but Tawana has pointed out that usually Partners get written up for this."

Being "written up" was terrible at Starbucks. I had never known any Partner who was fired, but I had heard that the process started by being "written up" for some infraction.

Almost as though following my thoughts, Crystal said: "You can be written up . . . especially for any financial situation. Eventually, enough write-ups on this kind of thing can get you fired."

I suddenly felt pure panic. Not fired! Not again. And especially now, not fired from the one place I felt safe and secure and, yes, loved.

I had a sudden vision of myself tossed out onto the bleak, gray January cement pavement of this cold city. I realized again how far I had come from my former external status supports of a big home, a big job, fancy suits, which I had sought to give me comfort, and which had failed me so miserably when things went wrong. . . . Now, I told myself, with a growing courage, I had found with Starbucks a better *reality* . . . not based on external status *symbols* but on a real feeling of confidence and support and genuine affection and even admiration for and from the Partners and the Guests. And Crystal. Crystal and Starbucks had saved me. Saved me from my pursuit of empty symbols, but also my anxiety about a fear-filled superficial life that hadn't been, in the end, helpful or even enjoyable for me.

Unlike Tawana or even Crystal, since birth I had been placed on an upward escalator reserved for those few affluent, properly educated, well-spoken and well-dressed peers who would never stop ascending. I had not voluntarily gotten off that easy escalator. . . . I had been pushed and then stumbled farther down . . . and no one seemed to have been able to help me or even really notice my great distress and basic needs.

Of course that was my fault. When I lost my footing, and was not ascending but descending — rapidly — I could not bring myself to tell family or even my closest friends how unhappy I really was. Or that I was broke. Such a shattering reality was never welcome in my world.

I had not been brought up to speak such terrible truths. My mother lived in the full bloom of New England optimistic denial. For her, everything was always for the best in the best of all possible worlds.

She couldn't even bear to tell me that my father had died.

I had gotten the call early in the morning just days after Christmas seven years earlier.

"We had the most wonderful Christmas," she began, her voice as usual full of a musical vitality. "Your father helped Emma put all her toys together." (Emma was my parents' youngest grandchild. At such occasions, the youngest were naturally the focus.)

"It could not have been a more wonderful Christmas, and your father was such . . ."

Her voice paused . . . unusual for Mother. She could speak in a kind of stream of consciousness aria that could last for many minutes.

"How is he?" I asked in routine way.

"He's sick. . . ."

"What's the matter?"

"He died." My heart dropped from my chest. "But it could not have been a better Christmas!" She ended on an upbeat, uplifting note.

My mother embraced the Episcopal prayer "for the means of grace and the hope of glory." But she did more than hope. She greeted every moment with a conviction that it *was* glorious.

"O, glorioso!" was her exclamation to any information I might convey.

I could say: "Gordon is coming for dinner."

"O, glorioso!" she would respond.

Or: "I will be over to the camp for a swim."

"O, glorioso!" she would exclaim. Mother lived her life with a kind of passionate decision to view each moment as an incredible gift that she'd been presented with. Like a polite young child on Christmas morning, she always made sure she was thankful for, and not critical of, anything that was given to her in her life. She also was careful to keep all bad news buried.

I had to learn from others in her family after I was well into my forties that her grandfather Henry Harris Barnard had committed suicide by jumping down a well. Or that her great-uncle Gates had shot himself to death. Or that another favorite uncle of hers had to be taken from the steps of the Harvard Club to be locked away for the rest of his life in an institution in upper New York State. Or that her only sister, Frances, also had to be institutionalized, when she was still just a child, and was never seen by any family members again. These terrible truths were never mentioned by her to me.

After her phone call that morning reluctantly revealing my father's sudden death, I immediately jumped in the car and drove over to be with her. But she didn't want to talk about what had happened. She certainly didn't want an autopsy, or any pursuit of the truth of what actually had occurred to cause my father's death.

I learned later — from others — that my father had felt a back pain, and he had very uncharacteristically gone to a hospital to be checked out. At that moment when he was being examined in the hospital, I think my father realized something was terribly wrong and willed himself to die. Another man might have fought for more time, even as a semi-invalid. But my father had watched his mother die an agonizing, yearlong death from cancer when he was just a seven-year-old child. One of his lifelong goals was not to inflict that kind of lengthy suffering on anyone.

"Shoot me if I get like that," my father would often say, usually in an embarrassingly loud voice, pointing to a doddering relative at a party. He had instructed me with that scary command from my earliest childhood.

My father lived in a kind of terror of losing his mind. Through his *mindful,* constant effort of will and talent he had been able to keep his mother's tragic death from drowning him in depression.

But he had to fight against the deep down current every day.

My father had developed his powerful version of denial of his constant pain: first through his writing, which became more and more optimistic and entertaining as he deliberately found more enjoyable subjects than the terrible truth and searing hurt of those traumatic early memories. Then he also escaped through his embrace of a larger public role as an articulate celebrity known for his ability to amuse.

Yet when I first saw my father after his death, his face had fallen into a kind of tragic Greek mask. The early tragedy he had experienced and fought so hard to overcome through a lifetime of proud and powerful denial had finally reclaimed his features. The terrified sadness of the little boy made to kneel by his mother and pray by her side for her, as she grew sicker and sicker from a ravaging cancer, was now clear to see. It was a face of unbearable, heartbreaking loss for, despite all his prayers, his mother had died and left him to face the world alone. Now his early, terrible loss was undeniable in the stark and tragic features of his face. My dead father showed the sad terror of loss that he must have felt as a child abandoned. Despite all his devoted efforts — he had lost the woman he had loved and needed most in the world.

My poor father! I thought. *How he had suffered!* No wonder, I now realized, he had embraced a flight from such a horrific reality. . . . No wonder my father was so eager to spare the family and me that kind of lingering death.

My mother and father were alike in the way they chose to die. My mother also chose a sudden death.

She had gone to a doctor and been told that she had an aneurysm.

"What does this mean?" my mother asked.

"You have a choice," her doctor said. "You could have an operation . . . which could be quite lengthy and difficult. It would take at least six months to recover. On the other hand, if you don't have the operation, you could go at any time."

"Perfect!" my mother had exclaimed with her usual positive force.

She died at Christmastime less than two years after my father. Mother was dressed up, getting ready to go to a concert at church. She was headed for glory. She looked so beautiful. I wish I could have held her before she died. I hope she knew how much I loved her and how much I miss her.

I was sad not to have had a chance to tell both my mother and my father how much I loved them before they left me so hurriedly.

I hope they knew I had done the best I could to make them happy while they lived. I still feel guilty for not doing *more*. I should have been with them at their deaths to express my love and try to comfort them.

Yet for all my love for my mother and father, and for all their love for me, I knew that if they were still alive they would probably have been unhappy and uncomfortable in many ways with my present job, and my current life.

Now that I was living alone, my parents would probably be angry at that idea and accuse me of being selfish. Whenever I was not willing to help them at a family party or other grand occasion, I was "selfish." They both needed me to be a happy performer in the happy play they had created, and nothing I ever did was ever quite enough for them.

They would also be puzzled and upset that I was *happy* to work serving coffee and finding such pleasure and friendship with people they would hardly notice. They would be surprised that Crystal and her Partners had become such good friends for me.

My mother and father would be very uncomfortable with what to them would have been a shocking truth: I was *satisfied* with my service job and my simple life. I could not live to make my parents happy anymore.

I could not deny the feeling of a growing happiness in my heart. This new, quiet, inner happiness kept catching me unawares in the midst of a rush of serving a big line at Starbucks. I also felt my happiness blossom in a kind of warmth in my heart in the nurturing silences and my lack of any real social life. No more fancy parties. I knew my parents would have wanted me to continue to join in with their view of a wonderful life in a perfect world lived at the highest reaches of the arts and society.

I no longer had the energy or the will for it.

Thanks to Crystal and Starbucks, I no longer needed it.

Crystal and Starbucks had freed me to be me.

Taking a deep breath and reminding myself how wise she had proved in all the time I had known her, I told myself that Crystal wouldn't just throw me out right now, just because Tawana was trying to get me fired.

And I was right.

For then Crystal smiled. Thank God.

"Look, Mike, I *could* write you up for this . . . but I don't want to ruin your excellent record."

Thank you, Crystal, I said silently to myself.

"You have done such a great job with meeting and greeting, and those Coffee Tastings . . . ," her voice dropped off, "but you do have to be better at managing your register."

"Maybe I talk to customers too much while making change," I suggested, truly searching for some way to make things better.

But just then Tawana appeared. She had not waited for Crystal to write me up. She was probably worried I would not be punished enough.

"Hi, Tawana," Crystal said. "I've spoken to Mike about the register."

"He should be written up," Tawana said. "Partners can be fired for stuff like this."

Crystal paused. She was a strong woman. I noticed for the first time that she had small, silver earrings on today. She was also stylish, no matter the pressures of her position having to manage the various Partners and all their work habits, and all their emotions. When other Partners made mistakes, I had watched her being firm but also fair.

"I know my job, Tawana," Crystal simply said.

Crystal's tone conveyed a feeling of calm finality to the subject. She was not the type to be pushed where she didn't want to go.

Tawana gave Crystal a look of rage and anger that she had often directed at me.

"Mike is going to do better. I'm sure he can," Crystal told her, giving me an endorsement I really appreciated . . . given the fact I was so insecure about handling any money issues.

"You don't have to go to *college* to do the *register*," Tawana said, and stormed away.

I knew just where that apparently irrelevant comment had come from. I knew that Tawana had graduated from college and could not believe she had to do such menial jobs as punching a cash register or pulling drinks at the espresso bar.

"Okay, Mike." Crystal turned to me, giving me a serious look. Crystal might have grown close to me, but I was not going to be let off the hook. "*Concentrate.* I know you can do it."

I headed back out front, relieved by Crystal's confidence in me, and by the fact she had not fired me, but still disturbed by how angry Tawana was with me. Yet I could understand why she felt that way. Just a *week* ago I had been reminded of the social and cultural divide that still separated me from the lives of most of my Partners in the way I lived my life outside my Starbucks store. I had come in for a mid-morning shift. When I went down the stairs, I saw Kester talking with Charlie. I thought he was helping him sort out his complicated love life. But it was much more serious than that.

It turned out that Charlie was sharing with Kester a scene he had witnessed on the way to work that morning. A younger sister of one of his girlfriends had gotten in an argument with another sixteen-year-old girl.

"They were yelling at each other and Julie

took out a knife, just to threaten her. But then the other girl kept yelling, and Julie took a stab at her, and the knife went right to her heart. It was an accident. But the other girl is *dead.* Two seconds, and Julie's life is over. I mean her fucking life is over."

Charlie's face was white, his voice was shaking.

Kester put his arm around him — a rare gesture.

"Sixteen years old, and her life is over," Charlie repeated. I had a sudden revelation of how far my world was from theirs. My streets in Bronxville were safe. I had never seen anyone stab anyone. Yet this was a grim and terrible reality most of my Partners lived with every day. No wonder Tawana was upset with me. From her point of view, I lived in a protected bubble of privilege, and it was about time I was given some hits. Tawana might not stab me, but she would be happy to see me get hurt in some way. She had been hurt by a world that was tilted against her. Wasn't it about time that I got what was coming to me? She certainly wasn't about to grant me any slack. Who had ever granted Tawana any slack? So I could understand Tawana's anger, and how she would want to take it out on me because she saw me as a representative of another

world that had kept her down. More remarkable was Crystal's attitude. Crystal had
grown up in the same tough world that was
tilted against her, but had somehow found
it in her heart to see me as a person —
rather than a symbol of a repressive society.

I couldn't help but conclude that part of
Tawana's rage at me was because I was an
old, white guy — part of the group that she
felt had oppressed her, and maybe I was the
kind of person who had turned her down
when she had applied for a job, optimistic
with her new diploma.

I could easily have been that jerk in the
past, I admitted to myself. But I was quietly
sure I wasn't that jerk now, and I thought
how unfair to me Tawana was being. The
rest of the Partners seemed to have accepted
me — despite our different backgrounds.
They considered me as their Partner in fact
and in name. Why couldn't Tawana do the
same?

Now Kester stopped me before I reached
the front of the store. He put a hand on my
shoulder.

"Lighten up, Mike. Tawana's like that with
everyone." He gave me his big smile. "Don't
take it personally."

That afternoon, I observed her from afar
and realized that he was right. Tawana

dissed all the Partners, and even some of the Guests. She had an inclusive hate. By the end of the day, I could understand that she wasn't attacking me, she was attacking everyone. And I felt genuine sympathy for her. How would I have felt if, after going to college, I couldn't get the job I had imagined for myself? I had been given a big job right out of college without lifting a finger. In that way I was a proper focus for her rage. She knew I had not suffered the way she had. No wonder Tawana was pissed. But from that moment, with Kester's advice ringing in my ears, I didn't take her rage *personally.* I was no longer the stuffed shirt I had been. I now proudly wore a Starbucks T-shirt, and knew in my heart I would do what I could to help Tawana, or any other Partner, to be as successful as they could be.

Not long after, I remembered how at J. Walter Thompson they had told me not to send "praise memos" because such positive missives could make them liable to a lawsuit if we had to fire the person.

In fact, once we had a special meeting at the corporation, in which the head of Personnel told us, "You will have to fire many people, so don't commit to them in print." We were encouraged to be as stingy as possible with any praise — especially any written positive comments. "They could come back to haunt us," the Personnel director intoned.

Now, at Starbucks I could freely, even sappily express how happy I was, and how much I appreciated my Partners. I started writing notes to other Partners for being so kind and helpful to me. I wrote Kester thanking him for his advice and leadership, and calling him a "great coach." I wrote a note to Bianca, saying her sweet smile meant a lot to me when I saw a long line waiting for me to call drinks and make change. I wrote to Joann telling her how her quiet, patient competence had helped me make it through the experience of doing everything for the first time.

I wrote Crystal, saying, in too few words, how much I appreciated not only her giving me a chance, but also her making sure I then succeeded in the new world I had joined.

"You are a true star in Starbucks," I wrote her.

I wrote Charlie the Music Man saying how much I appreciated his upbeat energy. "There was many a night, Charlie, where your positive attitude was as great an uplift as a great cup of coffee."

I also sent a note to Anthony: "Your class, from your steady, graceful smile to your shoes always shined so bright, adds a warm light to all our lives."

It was such a relief to me to truly express my positive emotions toward my Partners.

I was not playing some corporate game; I was expressing my honest feelings on paper.

I followed this up by doing a Partner poem each time someone had a birthday. And during the holidays I did an appreciation for the Partners:

"*You* are the Greatest Present
Just by being present.
With your cheerful spirit you are a precious, wondrous gift.
You bring warm welcomes to every busy shift.
You bring us new happiness every single day.
You make our work a form of joyful play."

I didn't stop with the Partners. Now I set my sights on the Guests to whom I was also grateful. With Guests, when it was their birthday, I would write them a little personal poem. For Denise, I would point out how much I enjoyed her brilliant scarves and chapeaus. For Dr. Paul, I would thank him for all the work he was doing to help little kids with arthritis. For baby Ella, I would say her early chirpings were as good as any songs by her namesake Ella Fitzgerald. For Rachel, I complimented her on Max: "The Maximum Baby."

For a guest named Jane, I wrote this bit of doggerel:

"Your wonderful smile
When you walk in the door
Helps to make
Our spirits soar.
You make sure to ask
Just how we are
When we see you at the register
Or at the bar.
Little wonder
You are *our* star
And a favorite Guest.
You bring out
Our very best!"

The poems weren't great works of art, but the Guests loved the personal appreciation. They loved it because it was from my heart.

I could be sincere at Starbucks because I was finally in a work environment that valued those precious moments of truly human interaction. From the moment when I admitted that I was so happy to be there, it had seemed so simple and easy. Why didn't *every* company work that way?

Because, I had to admit, it cost money. JWT fired a lot of people when they were no longer "cost effective." They had fired *me.* Most companies didn't want to really give their people decent health benefits. . . . It cost too much money. No other company I knew gave part-time people such incredible benefits.

And stock.

Constant recognition and new ways to learn — I thought of all the attention and recognition that I had received since I had walked in the door.

The company's respect was backed up by costly investments in me and every Partner. So Starbucks *was* unique. Probably always would be.

I didn't want to risk losing my job. The register was my least favorite activity; I had known it would be, but it was an essential part of the job. I could not treat it as casually as I had.

From that day when Tawana had tried to get me fired, I did *concentrate* on the register. I made conversation a little less. Since I saw the world in pictures and words, rather than numbers, I developed a trick to keep my mind straight. I'd call out the face on every bill I was given. I would call, out loud, Abraham Lincoln if I was given a five-dollar bill, or Alexander Hamilton for a ten, Andrew Jackson for a twenty. By calling them out, I was forced to fill my mouth and mind with words that had nothing to do with conversing with the Guest in front of me, and everything to do with concentrating on where I was putting the money. In addition, when I handed back the change, I would call the amount out loudly to the Guest: "Four dollars and sixty-five cents."

I must have sounded like a carnival barker with my exaggerated and loud calling out of every transaction. Gradually, I became more confident and started to instinctively focus on the money, allowing me to continue with those conversational interactions I'd enjoyed so much before.

About two weeks after Crystal had talked with me, I added up my register in her office. She was on the phone, ordering more supplies; I was totaling it up on the weighing machine. This was always a moment of reckoning for me, and I faced it with trepidation every time. I punched a button on the computer. Voilà: The screen showed that I had taken in over $840, and I was just three cents over. Just *three* cents! That would be an excellent effort for anyone, even Tawana.

I couldn't resist bringing my great achievement to Crystal's attention.

When she got off the phone, I proudly exclaimed, "Look, I'm only three cents over!"

She glanced over and nonchalantly said, "Great. I knew you could do it, Mike."

To her, it seemed it was no big deal. I couldn't believe it. But then I realized with surprise that it hadn't been that big a deal for her because, unlike me, she had never been worried about me, or my ability.

Crystal had more confidence in me than I had in myself.

Over the next days, I overheard her telling other Partners they should follow my example in engaging our Guests in conversations.

One day as I was cleaning up the condiment bar after doing one of my Coffee Tastings, I heard Crystal call to me.

"Mike," she said, "have you got a minute?"

I turned.

She was with a man who was smiling.

"This is Abe. I have told him how great you are."

How great I was, I thought, nice words to hear.

I made sure there were enough napkins on the bar; I didn't want to screw up now.

"You're due for a ten-minute break," Crystal continued. She seemed to always have my schedule, everyone's schedule, clear in her head. How did she do it?

"Yes," I said, finishing with the napkins and checking to make sure there was enough sugar. I had found at Starbucks that you worked while you talked. There was always something more to do. Guests took handfuls of napkins; they used up incredible amounts of sugar. Sometimes I thought we were selling napkins and sugar more than coffee! I had begun to feel a personal responsibility for the shape of the store. To run out of napkins or sugar made me feel bad.

As I listened to Crystal, I continued working, now wiping down the counter and cleaning up the condiment bar.

"During your break, Mike, I'd like you to sit down with Abe. He's our new district manager and he wants to meet our Partners."

"Sure," I said, happy to share my break with . . . Abe. Long ago, I had heard that it was easier to remember someone's name if you linked them with a visual image. From all my intensity at the cash register, the visages of our former presidents were ingrained in my mind — they even floated in my dreams as I fell asleep at night. I had a handy visual image for Abe: a five-dollar bill. Abe Lincoln, I told myself. A few minutes later, I joined Abe (Lincoln) and Crystal at a table in the back of the store. Crystal got up.

"I'll leave you two alone," she said. "I've got a lot of work to do."

I really looked at Abe for the first time. He seemed to be in his late thirties.

"Mike," he said with a warm smile, "Crystal says you are one of the best at delivering legendary service." Legendary service was Starbucks shorthand for making positive connections with the Guests through conversation and extra efforts to serve them.

"I enjoy talking with the Guests," I responded.

"That's great. This is definitely a people business."

"And I love the coffee," I said spontaneously. For some reason, I felt I could trust Abe. You know how you meet someone and you feel right away that you don't have to pretend? Abe had a kind of tangible, relaxed confidence that immediately set me at ease. I also felt he was prepared to believe the best of me.

"I love coffee too," he said. "I grew up on a coffee farm in Costa Rica. My family grows coffee."

"How did you get to Starbucks?" I asked.

"I worked for Pepsi, then went out and had my own business. A wine business. But I'm happy to have discovered Starbucks."

Discovered Starbucks, I thought. *What a great way of describing it.*

"Then you can really appreciate how unique Starbucks is," I said.

Abe laughed.

"Absolutely. This is the best place I've been."

"Me too!" I said.

Abe smiled.

"How did you get here?" he asked.

"A random act of kindness," I said. "Crystal offered me a job."

Abe laughed again. It was like we were old friends sharing a wonderful, true story.

"Where do you live?" Abe asked, then said, "Crystal says you are really dedicated, giving us *total availability,* and yet you have a long commute."

"Total availability" was Starbucks talk for being willing to go to work at any hour of the day or night. I had signed up for "total availability" when I first met Crystal and she had helped me fill out my job application. I had learned since that Crystal and every Starbucks manager really liked baristas who could be available around the clock. Many experienced baristas gradually asked for "no openings" or "no closings" or "no weekends." I felt that I might be able to do that eventually, but this first year I knew I would have to offer flexibility. And I still felt that way. Especially since I still didn't really know what I was doing. I felt that Starbucks was still more valuable to me than I was to Starbucks. So I gave my life completely — physically, mentally, and emotionally — and promised, verbally and in writing, that I would be available whenever they needed me.

My other priority, aside from Starbucks, was my children. I tried to see Jonathan as often as time allowed, which usually meant once or twice a week. My daughter Annie was living in Brooklyn, so she came by and I could see her more easily. Once, she starred in an off-Broadway show just a few blocks away from the store, and I was able to go see her in it on opening night. She was really great. Annie played a kind of crazy, angry woman — a role she threw her heart into. Even when she was in elementary school, Annie was a showstopper in any production. She could just walk onto the stage and the audience would shift in anticipation in their seats. They knew that she had a great gift for projecting true emotions. She had played Antigone in college to rave reviews, so this off-Broadway show featuring a tortured soul was perfect for her.

My oldest daughter Elizabeth had called herself Bis because when she was small, she couldn't pronounce her full name. In a sense, she gave herself her name, which was appropriate. Bis was always a creative force, writing and doing original artwork when she was young, writing and directing films as she got older.

Bis had stopped in once, and I had introduced her to Crystal and several other Partners, but she and I stayed in touch primarily through e-mail. She had always been very loving and supportive of what I was trying to do . . . although she had also expressed her concern with how I had upset my life. But now that I was on my own, struggling to start a new life, she was right there with me. I told her in an e-mail that I felt bad I had not been a better father, and she wrote back: "I have always felt loved, and you have been a great dad."

That made me feel good.

My daughter Laura was away at college most of the year. Once or twice, when I had two days in a row off, I went up to see her. She had come down to the city a couple of times to visit friends and see me, although she hadn't had a chance to meet Crystal. We went out with her friends. Laura, whom I called Loda, always had a gift for sympathy; she was sympathetic with me, although she was sad that "I don't see more of you anymore." That made me feel guilty. I felt bad I couldn't see more of my kids.

My son Charles was also away at school, but I had made a point of going to see him sometimes when he played soccer or lacrosse and spending his birthday with him and some of his friends and taking him to a Red Sox game (his favorite team). I would also go up to see him whenever else I could — although those occasions had been few in the last year since I had started my Starbucks job.

Aside from Starbucks and my kids, I hardly did anything. I would go back to my little apartment and make a simple meal of a bowl of cereal or open a can of tuna fish. During my "meal break" when I was working in the city, I would run across the street to a twenty-four-hour diner. There I would treat myself to scrambled eggs and bacon or a turkey sandwich. During a meal break we only had half an hour to eat, so I didn't have much time to savor any food.

Yet my total availability to Starbucks was a kind of gift for me. The challenging work, the daily struggle to learn and get things right, filled my life with so much stress and activity that I was hardly ever lonely. I approached the job at Starbucks as a question of survival, and I was totally engaged. I had no time to feel sorry for myself, and even the guilt I felt at hurting others was mitigated by my focus on doing well each day in this challenging job.

So the "total availability" I had given to Starbucks had helped to save me from myself and my anxious thoughts of past and future.

Abe was looking at me, and I realized I had not answered his question about where I lived. Sometimes, even in such important interactions, my mind would wander. Was this a sign of growing old, a "senior moment"? I could not claim such an easy dispensation — for I had always been a dreamer. Once, years ago, a colleague from work had seen me walking along, and called my name. I went right by him, not out of malice but just the fact that I was entirely in my own world and hardly saw where I was walking, let alone any other person. Retreat to my own dreams had been a way I had survived the early loneliness of childhood, and it was hard to give up that habit of escape — even when talking with a person like Abe.

What was his question? I asked myself. *Oh, yes, where do I live? That's what Abe had been asking!*

"I live out in Bronxville," I said. "It takes me an hour to make it here." It was really about an hour and a half, but I didn't want to make a big deal of it with Abe.

"Bronxville?" Abe said. "We have a store in Bronxville."

There was silence. I knew about the Bronxville store. I could see it from the train when I hurried into the city. And I had actually gone in for a Latte from time to time.

"You know," Abe said, "Starbucks believes in Partners working close to their communities. That's one of our uncompromising principles. Community involvement."

"Good idea," I said, without thinking.

"Have you ever thought of working in Bronxville?"

"But I love my Broadway store," I said, once again without thinking.

"Yes." Abe smiled. "And it's clear that Crystal and the other Partners love you. It's up to you," Abe said, "but you might want to think about working in a store closer to your home at some point."

"I *do* know the village of Bronxville," I said. "I went to school there."

"Exactly," Abe said. "But just think about it. At Starbucks we like to help our Partners lead the life they want. Whatever makes the most sense for you. I'll support *your* decision," Abe said, looking at me seriously. "Whatever decision you make, Mike, I will make sure it happens."

What a great endorsement. I really appreciated Abe's backing. Of course, Crystal had set it up, but Abe was clearly an honest person. I appreciated his confidence that I would make the right decision.

I remembered how at J. Walter Thompson they had called me in one day and said: "You're going to work in LA."

Or: "You're going to work on Ford."

It was never a question of what was best for me. I never remembered them ever asking my opinion about any assignment. Or given me any time to consider options. Here, at Starbucks, even as a relatively new Partner, Crystal and the "upper management" were most concerned that I did what *I* wanted to do.

Crystal came back to the table.

"You two getting along?"

Abe laughed.

"Great," Abe said.

"Now I'd like you to meet Joann, Abe. She has been with us for more than three years . . . one of the most experienced Partners."

I got up and Joann sat down.

It would be several weeks before Abe's words would reverberate to change my life at Starbucks.

9

CRYSTAL TAKES ME
TO THE BAR

"They told you that beauty is in the eye of the beholder. What they failed to tell you is that what you look like isn't important. What is important is who you are inside and the choices you are making in your life."
— a quote from Tiana Tozer, 1992 silver and 1996 bronze Paralympic medalist, women's wheelchair basketball, published on the side of a cup of a Grande Skim Latte

February
Over a series of weeks, Kester had been preparing me to get ready to make a move to "the bar," meaning I would make the drinks themselves. The bar was the next step up in the Starbucks hierarchy. It was like going from waiter to head chef. At the bar, you were responsible for delivering Starbucks drinks exactly right — with the cor-

rect temperature and weight of espresso and steamed milk.

Kester had shown me how to make sure a thermometer was always in the mug in which you steamed the milk.

"It should be between 160 and 180 — never more," he said. He had also instructed me in how to clean out the mugs, to keep the milk fresh. Then he had given me different tests when we had a few moments without Guests. "Make me a Grande Upside Down Caramel Macchiato," he would call out. When I had made the drink, he would take its temperature and weigh it to make sure it had the right proportion of milk and espresso. Once he called out, "Venti Soy Extra Dry Cappuccino."

I hurried to get a mug of soy milk ready. I had learned you should always have the milk ready before you drop in the shot of espresso. Espresso has a short life of great taste, so it should be as fresh as possible when served to a Guest. That meant that you should steam the milk first so you can add it immediately to the espresso.

I tried to steam the soy milk into a frothy, foamy mixture. A cappuccino was basically frothy milk, on top of shots of espresso, yet with the soy milk it was hard to get the proper "head." It didn't seem to want to froth up. And then, suddenly, the soy milk almost erupted out of the mug, spilling all over the bar. I had steamed it much too hot trying to get it to foam up.

I could hear Kester laughing. Charlie also came over to join in the fun.

"It's hard to steam soy up for a cappuccino," Kester said, hitting me on the back.

"Especially an Extra Dry Soy Cappuccino," Charlie joined in. "That's got to be the toughest drink."

"Shall I try again?" I asked, smiling but worried I had failed some major test.

"Forget it, Mike," Kester said. "Almost no guests order that, and I'll help you if they do. Now just make a regular Tall Cappuccino."

I steamed up some frothy whole milk for a Tall Cappuccino, dropped in a shot of espresso, and gave it to Kester to take its temperature and weigh it.

"Perfect, Mike," he said with a big smile.

I was relieved as well. Each drink to me was still a big challenge. There seemed to be so much to remember. And since I had never been much interested in cooking, I was also not much good at being exact — like with temperatures and stuff like that. The bar was still a high-anxiety area for me.

312

Now, as I struggled into my green apron, Crystal asked me, "Mike, could you jump on the bar today?"

It was an offer I could not refuse. While I wasn't sure I was up to the challenge, it was a chance to leave the dreaded cash register. Crystal smiled as she saw my hesitation, and moved down to the espresso bar to help me fill the orders.

While Kester had shown me the various combinations and how all the machines worked, it had been during slow times. Now we were in the midst of an afternoon rush, with Crystal, whom I desperately wanted to please. With her watching, any confidence I had quickly left me. Today the espresso bar itself seemed like a gleaming silver monster, capable of belching powerful steam to heat milk or dropping hot, black espresso shots — but also capable of going crazy with spluttering rage at the tentative touch of an inexperienced hand. I had never had a way with machines, and they always seemed to sense it. And I *was* inexperienced.

After heating my third jug of steamed milk, I turned too fast, hit it against the side of the espresso machine, and it poured unto the floor.

Crystal ran and got a mop. She was laughing.

"It happens to everyone," she said.

Despite her encouragement, I was embarrassed.

It took me many more weeks just to *begin* to get it right. Sometimes I would forget to make the coffee Decaf for a particular Guest, and I would have to start the drink all over again. Once or twice, concentrating on the milk and vanilla syrup ingredients, I forgot to drop in the espresso, and the Guests returned to the bar counter wondering why there was no coffee in their drinks.

I was finally getting into the flow of making drinks — into a kind of focused concentration where all that mattered was making them right at the right time. I could easily handle a call for a Grande Skim Latte, followed by a Tall Caramel Macchiato and a Doppio or a Venti Two Pump No Whip Mocha. I was in the zone. As the drinks were called, I executed with intensity and perfection. I had put two Tall Skim Lattes and one Grande Caramel Macchiato up on the bar. When I looked up to make sure they were taken by the right customers, as sometimes guests mixed up their drinks, to my shock I saw Charles, Laura, and Bis staring back at me. I did a double take, and then they all laughed.

"I didn't recognize you for a moment," I said.

"I recognized you!" Bis said.

"I've got a meal break in five minutes," I told them.

"Great."

They took their drinks and headed over to a table.

When I joined them, they were laughing together at some joke. I was pleased they all seemed to get along so well . . . especially now, when they were all getting so grown up. And especially since I had inflicted such pain on all of them. It was a rationalization to help ease my guilt, but I told myself at that moment: At least they have one another!

My kids were in the city to see the opening of Bis's new film, *Goldfish Memories*. And now Bis led the way in approving of my new job.

"I love this," she said, glancing around. "This is perfect for you." Bis was in her thirties and the eldest of my kids. She was happy in the life she had created for herself making movies in Ireland, and I felt she was the most open to this new version of mine.

At that point, Crystal came over. It was clear she wanted to see whom I was sharing my meal break with. Crystal had grown so close to me in recent months that she was no longer shy about inquiring what was going on in my private life. We had also talked about my children, and she had said I should "bring them in." She had already met Annie and Bis on previous visits.

I stood up and introduced Crystal.

"She runs this whole place. . . . She is my boss."

My daughter Laura, who had not yet met her, seemed tickled to see I was working for Crystal.

Laura and I had had many fights about affirmative action over the dinner table when she was growing up. Even though she was now at college, she had not lost any of her sympathy for people less fortunate. I had learned much too late that there were many people of a different color or lack of educational opportunities who could meet or exceed my achievements if given half a chance. Like Crystal, and virtually every Partner at Starbucks. I was, even now, certainly not even the best at doing my job. Maybe I had — after months of serious struggle — made it to the *middle* of the pack.

It was clear that Laura was pleased I was finally "getting it." And very happy that Crystal had now become my boss.

"Don't let him get away with anything,"

Laura told Crystal.

Laura didn't need to worry! Crystal shot back with a smile, "I *don't* let him get away with anything."

And they both cracked up into laughter — at my expense.

Then Crystal made a point of shaking hands in a kind of formal way with all my kids.

"Mike's doing good," she said, smiling toward me. "And your father is *funny*," she said. "We all like working with him."

Laura and my other kids smiled. I'm sure they had probably thought of me as a pompous ass on many occasions. It was probably a surprise for them to hear that I was accepted.

Then Kester swung by the table. "You got a call," he told Crystal. I introduced all the kids again. Kester didn't say anything, just gave them all a big smile, and that was more than enough. I felt that they really loved Kester at first sight, and he had, in a sense, endorsed me just by showing up and being so comfortable with me.

"Good meeting you," Crystal said to my children, and left with Kester to take her phone call. Crystal had a thing about always being available to anyone . . . even anyone on the phone. "Part of my job is not to let anyone down," she told me once.

I was happy Crystal was so relaxed with my children . . . just as she had become with me.

When Crystal left, I turned to my eighteen-year-old son, Charles, still just in high school; he was usually pretty quiet, especially around me. I was worried that of all my kids Charles would have the hardest time with my being a barista at Starbucks. It was not the kind of job you could boast about to your adolescent friends. My father had given me a wonderful car when I'd first gotten my driver's license. That was the kind of thing young teenage guys could admire. I could not do anything like that for Charles. I felt guilty.

Yet Charles had assured me, in a quiet way, over the last months when I had talked to him and deliberately brought up the subject, that he was fine. Charles had always had a kind of serene style and a cheerful acceptance of life that was foreign to me.

"What do *you* think, Charles?" I asked him.

"Can you get me a Starbucks card?" he asked. Bis and Laura laughed, and I joined in.

"Yes," I said, smiling.

"Cool," he said. I could imagine Charles

being happy to offer his friends some free drinks. Maybe, because Starbucks itself had become so popular among even high school kids, my working there was not a total social disaster for him. It was entirely likely that I was projecting my former social ambition and previous anxiety about losing my social standing onto my son — and to him, maybe it was a non-issue.

I *was* proud of my job, I reminded myself, and the good job I was doing.

Charles could see that I was working hard. Maybe that was enough.

I looked at my watch.

I didn't want to be late getting back from my meal break. Starbucks was like a sport in the sense that every shift was carefully calibrated with just the right number of players on the field at one time. If you were late coming back from a break, you hurt some other Partner, waiting to get off the field for a few minutes.

I made plans to meet again with my children later that night when I got off work.

I stood up.

All my kids stood with me, then put their arms around me and gave me a great circle hug.

I felt better as I headed back toward the espresso bar. As it had been when my daughter Annie first visited me, none of them seemed embarrassed. What a great relief. Maybe they were putting up a brave front for my sake, but I sensed that they were sincerely happy that I was working hard at making my life better.

I hurried back to get on the espresso bar, but Crystal gestured for me to follow her back to her little office.

Despite my best instincts, the old fear of failure nagged at me once again. I had missed a lot on my way to being fired at J. Walter Thompson. I no longer trusted my "instincts." Had I done something wrong? Crystal had seemed so relaxed with me in recent months, and with meeting my children just now, yet I might very well have missed something.

Crystal smiled, seeing my concerned face. Crystal always seemed to know just what I was thinking. How had she gotten so bright so young?

"Your kids are great, Mike." She laughed as we headed into the office. "You are really Mr. Lucky."

"True," I said, realizing that she was so right. It wasn't what *I* had done, or what *I* had failed to do. They were simply good kids. Luck had played a huge role. I hadn't taught Bis to read or love to work. I hadn't ever talked with Annie about how to project true emotions to a huge audience. I had not instructed Laura about how unfair life could be if you weren't born at the top. I had never coached my son Charles to have a graceful, serene temperament. And as uptight and time-conscious as I was, I could never have encouraged Jonathan in his great talent for enjoying the moment. My kids had all been unexpected and undeserved gifts to me.

Despite everything I had stupidly done, and left undone, somehow my children were decent and seemed willing to forgive me. I felt deeply grateful to my children's understanding hearts.

And for being here with Crystal. It was all part of the puzzle, the mystery of what was happening to me. Had my working for Crystal at Starbucks helped my children to forgive me? I knew it wasn't that simple.

Crystal sat down in the office.

"Sit." She gestured to the small chair next to her.

"Nothing bad," she said, quickly, realizing that I might think I had committed some infraction. "Just want to talk."

She turned toward me. I noticed she had her hair tied back, and the Starbucks hat on her head almost looked like a great fashion statement. Somehow, Crystal gave everything she wore a feeling of enhanced glamour.

"I've been thinking about what Abe said."

Abe? For a minute I could not remember who he was . . . a Guest? Then I quickly placed him. That kind man with a gentle smile . . . the new district manager who had said he would help me in any way he could.

"About the move to Bronxville," Crystal said.

"I told him I loved *your* Broadway store," I said quickly. This conversation was not going where I wanted it to go.

"I know. That's what Abe said. But I've been thinking about it. What is your commute?"

"About an hour?"

Crystal gave me a look.

"About an hour and a half," I confessed.

"That's long, Mike. Anthony has the second longest. Almost an hour. But I live twenty minutes away, and you know Kester is up at One Hundred Twenty-fifth Street."

"Yes" was all I could say.

"The commute has got to cost you . . . what . . . over a hundred bucks a month?"

"More," I said, being honest. Why lie? Crystal would know. I had given up even trying to hide or lie with her. Even from our very first meeting. In some ways, she knew me better than I knew myself. She had proved that. Another reason I didn't want to leave her.

"So the Bronxville move would make *time* sense and *money* sense for you. Plus, Starbucks has a principle of community involvement. You do a great job here, Mike, and you can stay, and you do a wonderful job of connecting with our Guests, but in Bronxville you could help the store and be more a part of the community where you live."

Crystal did things by the book. I knew that Starbucks principles such as community involvement meant a lot to her. Hadn't she taught me and showed me how the principles of dignity, respect, and diversity worked? These weren't casual words to her, but a guide to daily behavior.

"Hey." She saw the sadness in my face. "You don't *have* to go. But moving is the Starbucks way. There are always new opportunities for all of us. Kester will probably move on and up. I might go someplace someday. I was in another store before; I might move . . . anytime."

My heart fell. I had counted on Crystal being here forever. Still, I could see she was right.

"Starbucks is always on the move." Crystal smiled.

I had to smile with her. It was true. People were always coming and going. This was a booming business. New stores were opened every day. Forty million Guests, and more lining up at the door. Even in our store during the last months I had noticed our business had increased. Starbucks was growing so fast, how could I expect Crystal to stay in one place?

What she said also made sense financially. I was barely able to support myself, going from week to week on rent and food. While the health benefits were great, including an insurance policy I had taken out through Starbucks, I didn't want to have to actually *use* them. It would be much less stress and strain to walk to work rather than ride the trains and shuttle and subway. I was physically just about making it now during the incredibly active shifts. If I could eliminate the three hours a day of commuting, it would give me a big break physically and mentally between every shift. I was always anxious to make the right train, catch the shuttle, and grab the right subway. I was proud I had been able to do that without being late or even sick for any shift, but it was never easy. There was many a night, climbing those steep subway stairs on the way back to Bronxville, that I had staggered a bit from physical exhaustion and the pain in my aching feet. At sixty-four I knew I should take it easy on myself if I could. Already I had a brain tumor, and aches and pains I didn't even want to admit to myself I had acquired as I got older. I didn't want to have anything more go wrong with my body. Starbucks was a kind of frantic sport — every Partner needed to move fast, with a manual dexterity. If you couldn't move rapidly, you let down the other Partners.

I definitely could do a better job of reaching out to the community in the village where I had gone to high school. So I could not deny I could do a better job not only for myself but also for Starbucks in Bronxville.

"Hey, Mike, don't worry," Crystal said, sensing my sadness. "I'll back you on anything *you* want to do. Whether you go, or stay. That's *your* choice. Frankly, I'd hate to lose you. The Guests would really miss you. The Partners would as well. You're fun to work with . . . you make it fun."

She paused.

"*I'd* miss you too," she said, smiling but with serious eyes.

I appreciated those last words. Crystal had

given me a lot of public praise in recent days . . . but those face-to-face words that she would miss me meant the most.

I felt sad and scared at the idea of leaving the safety of what had become a life raft for me, but what Crystal now said made sense.

And Crystal was clearly glad at the opportunity to help me once again.

10
EXIT BROADWAY

TO MIKE
FOR ALL THE TIMES YOU HAVE STOOD BY US, WE THANK YOU. FOR SHOWING US WHAT LEGENDARY SERVICE TRULY MEANS, WE APPLAUD YOU. YOU HAVE TAUGHT US NEVER TO GIVE UP OUR DREAMS. THAT ONE DAY THEY COME TRUE. THIS IS OUR PRAYER FOR YOU.

Dear Lord please give him
- A few friends who understand him & remain his friends
- A work to do which has real value, without which the world would be poorer
- A mind unafraid to travel, even though the trail be rough
- An understanding heart

- A sense of humor
- Time for quiet, silent meditation
- A feeling of the presence of God, the patience to wait for the coming of these things, with the wisdom to recognize them when they come.

May God continue to guide you, Mike. We love you.

From all your Partners
at 93rd & Broadway.

— from a prayer written for me on last day working with Crystal and my Partners

March

My last shift did not start until one p.m. It was already noon at my little train station in suburbia, yet I knew I could make it to my store in New York City in plenty of time. I leapt onto the express train into Grand Central, ran to the shuttle to Times Square, jumped into the Number 3 subway on its way up to Ninety-third Street. I was now able to take all these frantic actions in a kind of Zen traveling zone. I hardly thought about every move — just went like a swimmer who gives up struggling and goes with the tide, borne along with the wave. Yet each forward motion this afternoon reminded me that this was my last day.

We had joked that our Starbucks store was the best show on Broadway. Now I would be moving *off* Broadway to a store right next to my apartment in Bronxville. Saving on the long commute was a good move for me, but by this time in my life, I knew that if you make an exit, it is never easy for you to make it back inside. I would return — sometimes — to say hello to my Partners at Ninety-third and Broadway, but I would never be working with them again.

While walking up the steep subway stairs toward the cloudy March light, I saw ahead, almost level with my eyes, the curious sight of a pair of Lobb shoes, the most expensive men's shoes in the world. I was shocked out of my zombie traveling zone. Lobb shoes are easy to spot. They give off a kind of inner light; the leather seems to shine like burnished gold. And the owners, inevitably, keep them polished to a high gloss. To get a pair, you have to travel to London and have Lobb take a mold of your feet. The shoes are then made to fit your unique measurements. Each pair costs several thousand dollars.

My eyes traveled from the shoes, up to the torso, bound tightly in a double-breasted blue suit with bold, chalk stripes that spoke of being handmade by a London tailor. Such a suit would cost even more than the shoes. Who would spend so many thousands on his personal appearance and yet ride the subway? Such shoes and suit usually were only found in a limo or at least a taxi.

As this overdressed man emerged with me into the dark gloom of the afternoon, I realized there was something about his awkward gait that I recognized. He moved with the exact same pugnacious arrogance of a classmate of mine at Buckley and Yale who was known to be incredibly rich and incredibly cheap: Everett Larkin Fallowes was one who would spend thousands on himself while riding the subway to save a few bucks on a tip for a taxi driver. He was notorious for never tipping anyone. He had actually gotten in a fight once with a taxi driver, and barely made it away with his life.

A year ago, I might have eagerly sought his company. Everett (as he asked his friends to call him) was a person who exemplified the highest status of my formerly secure past. Before my job at Starbucks, I would have reached out to him in my insecurity as a needed reminder of my old life. Yet today, of all days, I no longer needed to visit the supposedly secure world

I had left.

I passed Everett to get inside my store. I had found that several former acquaintances did not recognize me if they happened to come into my West Side store, which was rare. With my black cap and green apron, I was virtually invisible to them. I had my Starbucks hat on now, and Everett Larkin Fallowes did not give me a second glance. As I brushed past him, I had the sensation that I was not just moving around him, but was moving beyond him, as I had already moved beyond other remnants of my past, more arrogant self.

I went past the bar and behind to the small office area. This space held memories now. I thought back to just days after I had joined my store, when I overheard Crystal talking on the phone about the presentation she was worried about giving. I remembered what a moment of transition it had been for me — and for Crystal. I recalled my bossy instincts, and how Crystal had made me aware that my advice wasn't welcome. And yet I remember not just her skeptical look when I had told her about KISS and the Three P's — but her look of real joy when she heard from the company president about her job well done. From that moment on, I was someone in Crystal's eyes. It was in this office where Crystal had talked to me about my move to Bronxville. When she had hugged me in excitement, I had hugged her back, tears springing to my eyes. I think it is true that the older you get, the more you cry. That's certainly true for me. Whenever JWT asked me to change my whole life and move to LA or Toronto or D.C., I had been delighted to go. It was a new challenge to create a new office in a new place. I loved the feeling. But now, an old guy who had just been given a new life, and made new friends, with a new job, I didn't want to leave this familiar scene.

"You don't have to go, Mike," Crystal had said, reading my mind, "but this is better for you."

"Yeah, I know . . . but I'll miss you."

"Me too," Crystal said, but at twenty-eight years old, departures are not sad. The future beckons, and always looks brighter.

I would miss Crystal immensely, her advice, her kindness, her referring to me as "a funny guy" to all the other Partners.

I looked at the daily schedule posted on the wall by the office: Crystal wasn't due to come in. I was very disappointed; I had wanted to say a proper good-bye. I also noticed that Kester, my first coach and mentor, wasn't due in until tomorrow. Even

Charlie, the Music Man himself, was going to miss my shift.

With so many Partners coming and going at every Starbucks store, I had been prepared for the fact that my leaving was not to be a major occasion. I knew I could return and see them all some other time. Still, I had grown so close to these Partners, and part of me ached that they hadn't worked their schedules to be there with me on my final day.

I went down to the basement to put on my green apron. The basement was where we kept the coffee beans and extra cups and bottles of syrup and uniforms. It was the only private place in the store, so you could change without being disturbed. On that last afternoon, I made my way up the stairs for my last shift with a heavy heart.

As I went by the bulletin board on the way into the bar, I noticed that a new "customer snapshot" had been posted. Crystal had written across the top: "Congratulations, Mike."

That was me!

A secret "customer" came in every few weeks to judge our performance and report back to the management of Starbucks. This "customer snapshot" had been taken when I had been working behind the bar. The key criteria were:

Do you make eye contact?
Do you greet the guest?
Do you thank the guest?
Do you initiate conversation?
Do you recognize a guest by drink or
name?

I had hit all the criteria, and the store had gotten five stars for "legendary service." Five stars were the highest, and I was aware our Broadway store had never won more than four before.

I was going out on an up note.

I moved to the front counter. Oops. Tawana was on the espresso bar. The one person I did not want to see today.

"Mike," she said, in her loud, bossy voice, "take the middle register."

I punched in at the middle of the three registers. I took the drawer, with its cash, back to the office to count it. Sure enough, $150. I brought the drawer back to the register and slammed it in like the other Partners did, with a sense of confidence. I had gotten better at this crazy cash business. There was already a line waiting at the other two registers.

"Hello, Bianca," I said to the Partner on

my left. She gave me a small, warm smile.

On my right was Joann. She looked over quickly and gave me a welcome with a cheerful call, "Come help!" Joann had always been so welcoming to me.

"*Focus,* Mike," Tawana called out, making sure I did not get too comfortable.

Before I had a chance to take the first customer, she called to me, "I'm joining the Marine Corps."

"Good," I called back. "You'll like that life." And I wasn't kidding. Having worked with the Marines, I knew Marines were passionate, just like Tawana.

"I'm going in as an officer," she called to me. "After I do Quantico."

"Good," I replied again. Tawana liked bossing people around and would have a chance in the Marine Corps to release her rage in a positive way.

"Can I help the next Guest?" I asked.

First in line was Dr. Paul. Like clockwork, he came in every morning for a Tall Cappuccino with a plain bagel and jelly. In the afternoon, he would ask for a Grande Skim Latte.

"Grande Skim Latte?" I asked him.

"Right, Mike." My memory for names had treated me well at this job. And Dr. Paul had always made a point of calling me by

335

my first name. Not just me but all the Partners. This was a neighborhood store, and the Guests liked the feeling of connection.

"Your last day?" Dr. Paul asked.

"Right," I said, surprised that he remembered. Over the last week or so I had been telling some of my favorite customers that I would be leaving.

"I'll miss you, buddy," he said.

"Me too," I said, "but I'll always have your book."

"Yeah, right," Dr. Paul laughed, "but you don't even have arthritis."

"You never know," I called as he moved down to pick up his drink at the espresso bar. Dr. Paul had written a book on how to live with arthritis and had given me a copy.

I remembered back to my first few days meeting him, and all the other Guests. Several of them had asked, "How are they treating you?"

"The best job of my life," I would reply. "How bad can it be to serve great coffee and pastries?" And I wasn't kidding. The fact that I was so happy to be at their Starbucks store serving them made them feel better.

I called out Dr. Paul's drink to Tawana at the bar.

"Grande Skim Latte," Tawana shouted back at me, slamming a cup under the espresso outlet. She did her job extremely well, and yet everything seemed to be done with a kind of focused fury. Let the bad guys watch out — warrior Tawana was on the way. Better them than me.

Next came Denise, looking beautiful as always in her funky hat. "How's the art business, Denise?"

"So-so right now. . . . Hope it will get better."

"Shall I get you a Half-caf Grande?"

"Than would be great, Mike, thanks."

"Good afternoon, Ella," I said, as Robert and his daughter, Ella, came in the door. Every day at this time father and daughter would show up. Robert had been a space salesman for *New York* magazine, but had become a house husband once Ella was born. His wife worked for Goldman Sachs.

"You're having a Latte, and a Warm Kid's Chocolate?"

"Right, Mike. Is it true you're going?"

I nodded. "Yes, it makes sense . . . to a store where I live."

"Ella, Mike is going to go to another store," Robert told his daughter.

"Bye, Mike," Ella said, with the bright upbeat attitude of a three-year-old.

"Bye, Ella, take care of your father."

"She sure will," Robert laughed, picking her up and heading down the bar.

I was sure there would be other neighborhood families I would get to know at my new store, but I would miss these two. I willed myself to take Ella's positive attitude. "Hi" and "Bye" were equally exciting to her. And should be to me.

"Hey, guys." I greeted the regular pack of young guys from Collegiate School. They were wrestling with one another as they came up to me, but stopped long enough to say, "Three Tall Mocha Frappuccinos and one Tall Java Chip Frappuccino."

One young man held out a Starbucks card.

"All on one?" I said, knowing the answer.

"No way," he said. "Come on, guys, get your money on the counter."

Each of the boys carefully counted out the change, and the leader of this young group totaled it up, accurate to the penny.

Behind the boys was Eleanor, her backpack loaded with papers to correct. She taught at a local public school and would correct papers while sipping her Earl Grey tea.

"I'll get your tea, Eleanor," I said. The register Partner always had to make up the tea. Grabbing a cup and hot water brought me into the space behind Tawana.

"Mike?" Tawana said. She was being more talkative than usual today.

"Yes?" I was cautious.

"This your last day?"

"Yeah."

"Look."

With a wet, white cloth she vigorously wiped the wands on the espresso machine that steamed the milk.

"Always keep the wands clean."

I almost laughed. Were those to be her last, best words for me? "Okay," I said, keeping my head down, concentrating on making the tea.

An hour later, when Tawana's shift ended, I can't say I was torn up to see her go. As she headed to the back, she bellowed, "Take over, Yvette!" She was not nice to anybody, I thought. Tawana pulled off her apron and cap, shook out her hair, and seemed to shake off me and everyone in the store as she headed out the door without saying good-bye. Just the way she always left, as though leaving everything far behind.

Yvette took over the bar. I immediately felt better. "Hey, Mike." She gave me a hug. "How're you doing?" she asked me, rubbing me on the back.

"Good. It's my last day."

"Oh?" Her hand dropped from my back. "I forgot. . . . That's too bad." She looked sad. I could understand why Yvette could forget. She was always moving so fast between her shifts at Starbucks and her work at school.

"Moving to a store nearer where I live," I told her. "I'll save money on the commute."

"Cool," Yvette said, "but I'll miss you. You're funny." She gave me a tight, long hug.

Funny. Again. Crystal's favorite way of describing me. This time I laughed out loud.

"Hi, Rachel," I said to the next Guest. "Decaf Grande Latte?"

"Skip the Decaf," Rachel said. "Give me the good stuff. I'm not pregnant anymore, Mike."

Rachel held up her tiny baby, who was beautiful.

"Grande Latte for Rachel," I called to Yvette, and heard her powerful echo.

I realized these Guests, the Rachels, Dr. Pauls, Denises, and little Ellas, all had become good parts of my life over the last year.

I worked hard the rest of the afternoon. The store was always busy with a wide diversity of types. Teachers. Students. Businesspeople on the run. People having meetings — from job interviews to school faculty. Many mothers with babies in strollers looking for a needed break. The store was a good place — somewhere between home and work — to have a break. The line of waiting Guests never stopped, and I was really too busy to dwell too much on it being my last day. One of the important gifts from my job at Starbucks was that it was always so hectic you couldn't think about anything but serving the customers. When I was working, there was no chance for interior ruminations. It had been like therapy for me.

Around five o'clock I was surprised to see Charlie the Music Man show up.

"Hey, Charlie," I called to him, "this is my last day. I want to say good-bye."

Charlie walked in a kind of dance up to me, gave me a high five, and said, "See you later."

Then he headed to the back of the store.

I felt better. At least I had a chance to say good-bye to Charlie. I had put him in touch with a guy I had known from years ago who was in the music business. Charlie said the guy was helping him do a "real professional CD."

Then, about quarter to six, just before I was going to pull my register and clock out,

Kester walked in with a big smile on his face.

He shook my hand, and then did about fifteen other things, ending with a head butt.

"Kester, this is great. I wanted to say good-bye."

"Okay," he said, and also headed for the back.

On the dot of six, Crystal showed up. Something started growing in my heart, a warm feeling of gratitude. I was beginning to understand. My best friends in the Partners were coming in from where they lived to be with me at the end of my last shift. This was very rare. You didn't visit the store if you weren't going to work.

Even Anthony showed up, a Partner who I had said was the real class in the place. Anthony lived way out in the Bronx, almost as long a commute as mine, but he always had his shoes polished to a perfect shine.

"Mr. Mike," Anthony called me. He had picked that up from another Partner. I pulled my register and went to the back.

There they all were. Crystal was at her chair, laughing at something Kester had said. Charlie was moving to the sound coming from his earphones. Anthony, six feet four and plus, was leaning against the wall with a gentle smile on his face. As I entered the room, they gave a little cheer. They watched as I finished up weighing the money. I was only a few cents off.

"Finishing strong," Kester said, and everyone laughed. "Hey, Mike," Kester continued, clearly the ringleader in this group, "what are you doing tonight?"

"Just going home."

"How about coming out to dinner . . . on us?"

I was deeply touched by the offer. "Sure," I said.

When we left our Starbucks, Kester pulled out a fancy little camera and insisted that we all take a picture in front of the store. The sky had cleared, and the red sun was just going down. Kester asked a passerby to take our picture.

"One more," Charlie called out. "The camera loves me."

I'm sure it did. I tried to count how many female Guests had asked me for Charlie's phone number over the last year.

Everyone was feeling good as we went to a bar around the corner. I had never eaten there, or entered there before, but Kester and the others were well known. They ordered the drinks and the food, and wouldn't let me pay for a thing.

Crystal threw herself into the party, laughing and shooting pool. I shot pool too, the first time in forty years, and did not make a complete fool of myself. Bianca joined us for the evening, and Joann came by — but only for a minute. She wasn't feeling well.

Time seemed to dissolve, and when I looked at my watch, it was already one a.m. Everyone else was still going strong, but I was not young like them. When they saw I was getting ready to go, Crystal stopped me. Kester, Anthony, Charlie, and Bianca were all talking at a table at the back of the bar, and Crystal shut them all up by standing up.

"I got something to say. You are a funny guy, Mike."

Everyone laughed, and cheered.

"You brought a lot of legendary service to us. . . . I'm serious . . . but more important, you brought yourself. We've got a poem I wrote for you."

"We all wrote," Charlie interjected.

"Yeah, but I did more," Crystal said.

"And I did nothin'," Kester said, "but I'll miss you, Mike. We had some great closings together."

Crystal read the poem, crying a little at the end. I had them all sign it. This was better than any diploma or award to me.

"Now I want to talk," I said.

"You always want to talk!" Kester said, and everyone laughed.

"Yes, and *you* saved my life. Kester saved my life one night."

Kester had told me not to mention what he did to the out-of-control customer with a knife; he had said that Crystal would kill him if she heard. So I shut up about that now. But I went on to tell them what I felt.

"Crystal, you and Kester and Charlie the Music Man" — laughter — "and Bianca, and Gentleman Anthony" — more laughter — "all my Partners, you have all saved my life."

I couldn't say any more. I went around shaking hands, and promising to come by often to see them. Kester and Charlie pounded me on the back — hard. Anthony shook my hand and said, "You've made a big difference in my life, man."

Bianca gave me a little kiss. "Take care of yourself, Mr. Mike."

Crystal did not say anything more, just gave me a strong hug that almost took my breath away.

Then I went out into the winter night, warmed by their love.

ACKNOWLEDGMENTS

To my old friend William Burr Lyon for reacting in such a positive fashion to the title of my book, and introducing me at once with such generosity of spirit to his great agent, Gillian MacKenzie.

Gillian was a true inspiration and invaluable guide to this successful adventure. Her intuitions and insights were incredibly acute, and often prophetic. Her focused energy and upbeat spirit were like a wind at my back.

Gillian, in turn, introduced me to her friend Erin Moore, of Gotham Books, who edited this manuscript with intelligence, sensitivity, and a rare but welcome wit.

Erin's friend and publisher, Bill Shinker, has also been a key creative contributor throughout and has always been there when needed with his wise and timely advice.

Other important contributors at Gotham were Jessica Sindler; Aline Akelis, who handled the foreign rights; Lisa Johnson, director of publicity; and Amanda Tobier, the marketing director. Gary Mailman made sure that everything was legal. And Susan Schwartz, managing editor, was vital in bringing everything together in just the right way. In fact, everyone at Gotham and at Penguin has exerted every effort to create a work of the highest quality.

Gillian also introduced me to Shari Smiley of Creative Artists Agency, who helped choose Tom Hanks and Gus Van Sant as the ideal creative people to bring my story to film. I have been blessed by working with the best.

Speaking of working with the best, this story would never have been possible without all my Partners at Starbucks and their great encouragement on a daily basis. I wish it were a long enough book to include *all* their amazing and dramatic tales. But I *do* want to thank by name at least *some* of the Partners who made and continue to make my every shift at Starbucks so stimulating and uplifting. They are, in alphabetical order:

Angela
Bryan
Bill
Carmela
Christa
Christian
Claudia
Clayton
Cynthia
Denahsa
Edwin
Gillian
Howard
James
Jim
Joy
Julian
Julisa
Justin
Kate
Kevin

Leanda
Leylani
Matt
Mark
Martin C.
Martin R.
Mike
Lakeisha
Molly
Nehemiah
Patrick
Paula
Ralph
Tamar
Tenaya
Tiffany
Toya
Velinda
Vera
William
Yolanda

I also want to thank my children, who have been so supportive during what has been a very difficult time for them; and my siblings, my family, and my friends. Once again, I am indebted to so many people, there are many too many to mention in this space. But I do want to give a special shout out to: Breda, and Elsie — who had the idea of putting the quotes from the Starbucks cups at the head of every chapter. Thank you, and thanks everyone, including all the loyal, cheerful Starbucks Guests, for all your help in creating my surprising new life.

ABOUT THE AUTHOR

Michael Gates Gill was born in Connecticut, the son of Anne Gill and renowned *New Yorker* writer Brendan Gill. Educated at Yale, he went to work at the J. Walter Thompson advertising agency. After twenty-five years as a creative director at JWT, he was fired. He tried to start his own consulting company, but the next years brought increasing professional and personal crisis. Entering his seventh decade, he was struggling to survive. Almost by accident, he was offered a job at Starbucks. He was able to step behind the scenes of one of the world's most intriguing organizations, where inspiring friendships were born and new life lessons were learned. Today he lives and works as a barista at a Starbucks in the New York area.